Collaborative Leadership

Dedication

To the uncounted children in an unknown future who
will benefit from our work today. But, especially to Amelia and
Lane who gave up more nights with Dad and weekend romps
than they should have so I could finish this book! And to Tina
who endured and held us all together . . . with love.

In Memory
Of Monsignor Jack Egan, who stoked the fires of
passionate public service on behalf of social justice.

Collaborative Leadership

Developing Effective Partnerships in Communities and Schools

Hank Rubin

Foreword by Martin J. Blank

CORWIN PRESS, INC.
A Sage Publications Company
Thousand Oaks, California

For information:

Corwin Press, Inc.
A Sage Publications Company
2455 Teller Road
Thousand Oaks, California 91320
www.corwinpress.com

Sage Publications Ltd.
6 Bonhill Street
London EC2A 4PU
United Kingdom

Sage Publications India Pvt. Ltd.
M-32 Market
Greater Kailash I New Delhi 110 048 India

Printed in the United States of America

Library of Congress Cataloging-in-Publication Data

Rubin, Hank, 1952–
   Collaborative leadership: Developing effective partnerships
in communities and schools / by Hank Rubin.
      p. cm.
   ISBN 0–7619–7891–7 (c)
   ISBN 0–7619–7892–5 (p)
   1. Community and school—United States.   2. Educational
leadership—United States. I. Title.
   LC221 .R83 2002
   371.2′00973—dc21

                                                    2001007180

      03 04 05 10 9 8 7 6 5 4 3 2

This book is printed on acid-free paper.

Acquisitions Editor: Robb Clouse
Editorial Assistant: Erin Buchanan
Copy Editor: Annette Pagliaro
Production Editor: Denise Santoyo
Indexer: Molly Hall
Cover Designer: Michael Dubowe
Production Artist: Janet Foulger

Table of Contents

Foreword

Reading the daily newspaper and listening to elected officials, the average citizen might easily conclude that our schools are the only institution in American society responsible for educating our children for adulthood and for participation in American democracy. The fact that children grow up in families, that families live in neighborhoods and communities, and that families and communities share responsibility for the education of our children and youth seems to be lost on many opinion leaders and policy makers.

This perception about the role of education is partly a result of the isolation of too many of our public schools from the communities they serve. Principals and teachers generally do not live where they work. Educators learn to manage their buildings but learn little about family and communities in their preparation and professional development experiences. Changing demographics exacerbate the gap between school and community. Today 87% of our teacher work-force is Caucasian, while the 2000 census tells us that 35% of our school-children are from ethnic/racial minority groups—and that percentage will continue to grow. Parents, especially those with low incomes, face increasing stresses in their lives, and too often find schools unwelcoming. This isolation serves neither the interests of students nor those of educators, families, and communities. Rather, research and experience suggest that deep and intentional relationships among school, family, and community can help to create the conditions for all children to learn and to succeed in schools. What are these conditions?

- Students are motivated and engaged in learning inside and outside of the classroom
- Schools offer high-quality curriculum and instruction through qualified teachers
- Basic medical, emotional, and physical needs of young people and their families are being met

- Parents or other responsible family members are actively involved in supporting and making decisions affecting their children's learning
- School buildings and neighborhoods are safe and the school climate promotes respect and support among school staff, young people, parents, and community residents
- Schools are viewed as part of the larger community and use community resources to provide expanded opportunities for learning and civic participation before, during, and after school hours

Schools cannot create these all of these conditions by themselves, nor should they be expected to do so. Rather, schools must collaborate with families and with the vast array of public and private agencies, neighborhood community groups, businesses, and civic institutions to create the conditions for student learning. In our work at the Institute for Educational Leadership, we call schools that do this community schools.

Creating and sustaining community schools requires not only a thorough understanding of the process of collaboration, but also the leadership skills to make collaboration work. It is here that Hank Rubin makes a particularly valuable contribution.

The collaborative process that Rubin outlines will help educators and leaders in other sectors understand and appreciate the nature of what often seems to be a messy endeavor, but is in fact an approach that will work if correctly implemented. Equally significant, the dimensions of collaborative leadership Rubin has defined will be very useful to people who want to assess their own collaborative skills, helping them to find ways to be more effective leaders and contributors in collaborative enterprises.

Educators face extraordinary pressure today as they seek to enable all children to learn. If they work more collaboratively with family and community, that task will be easier and public support will grow for public education. Reading Hank Rubin's book and applying its lessons will strengthen their capacity to move in that direction.

Martin J. Blank
Director, School/Family Community Connections
Institute for Educational Leadership
Staff Director
Coalition for Community Schools

Preface and Overview

A few years ago, someone introduced me to an audience of educators as president of the Institute for Collaborative Learning. At the time I was heading the Institute for Collaborative *Leadership*, but it got me thinking. A collaborative leader is, in fact, a collaborative learner . . . and vice versa. If you're an effective collaborative leader, you learn about your partners in order to lead them, just like a good teacher learns about each student in order to teach him or her. The more we learn about others, the more collaborative, responsive, and linked to self-interests will be the work we can do with our partners.

The old adage is true—we must first understand if we hope to be understood.

So I began that speech by noting that there is a reason why everything any effective supervisor, manager, or leader needs to know is gathered in the skill pack of every excellent teacher. Excellent teachers connect instructional systems to learners one child at a time. They not only know what must be learned but also look at learning through the eyes of each young child they teach. And they take responsibility for their students' learning through planning, practice, tools, and partnerships. Effective collaborative leaders connect their institutional systems to the people with whom they work, one individual at a time, learning enough about the individual and the group to lead systemic change by influencing people collectively and individually. Effective collaborative leaders are clear on the goal they aim to achieve and succeed by learning to see that goal through the eyes of those they lead. And they take responsibility—become the "institutional worry"—for leading their partners collectively toward their shared goal(s).

This is a book for people who dedicate their careers or volunteer their time trying to make a difference in public matters . . . particularly those working to shape the future by improving the lives of children and families. This book grew out of my earlier work *Collaboration Skills for Educators and Nonprofit Leaders* (1998) and is expanded and revised by the comments, observations, recommendations, and lessons offered in connection with hundreds of collaborations and leaders in schools, communities, businesses, and universities across the nation.

This is a simple book intended to help leaders lead, teachers teach, and intellectuals think more effectively with and about collaboration. This book does not cull its management and leadership lessons from presidential campaigns, sports dynasties, dramatic corporate mergers, or public projects of the magnitude of the Tennessee Valley Authority or the Manhattan Project. Not that the concepts and skills we will discuss do not apply to these large complex operations; rather, these grand contexts are simply too distant to feel relevant for most of us who work and volunteer in the public sector. Besides, the size of institutions in which we operate has little bearing on the basic (human) relationship-management skills that collaborative leaders must master in order to make a difference.

Therefore, this book is geared toward the familiar workaday world of people in the big and small systems that touch the lives of children, including schools, districts, service agencies, volunteer organizations, and families.

At the heart of this book is the premise that meaningful public engagement and broadly inclusive participation in public education are virtues. Moreover, it is the responsibility of education's leaders to find ways to build and maintain mutually accountable partnerships with every able adult who can contribute to the success of public education. This book is written to be a tool for such public leadership.

First and foremost, this is a book for teachers, educational leaders (in school districts and nonprofit and government agencies), staff members and volunteers, university faculty, and students preparing for any of these positions. It is a practical exploration of what it takes to form and focus the collaborative *relationships* necessary to accomplish important public missions, particularly education. It is a book about *building villages*.

But be warned: This is more a *book of concerns, theories, and models* than it is a *book of answers*. By trying to identify and clarify the elements and phases that are part of collaboration, and by trying to create logical models for interpreting, doing, and evaluating collaboration, my aim is twofold:

1. To help practitioners improve their capacity and performance

2. To begin a dialog involving practitioners, educators, and scholars that will generate more and better answers, models,

and theories aimed at advancing the art of collaboration to the status of a science and a system that we can study, teach, learn, and improve

Essentially, this book has two parts. Chapters 1 through 4 look at the context, reasons, and complexities of collaboration from a number of perspectives . . . and pose a variety of arguments for *doing* collaboration. Chapters 5 through 9 attempt to respond to these arguments with explorations of how to *do* collaboration. Chapter 5 lays the groundwork for developing explanatory models of collaboration and connects collaboration to systems change. Chapter 6 introduces the 12 phases of collaboration's life cycle with a tool and framework to both assist practitioners and invite applied study. Chapter 7 introduces content skills and attributes that contribute to effective collaboration. Chapter 8 integrates practice and theory in a descriptive model of collaborative systems. Finally, Chapter 9 singles out a few nuggets of advice for those readers looking for pithy guidance right away!

Building Relationships for Children

As a nonprofit practitioner and educator for over 25 years, I encourage readers from the third sector to look for the relevance of this book's discussion of skills and principles to the work we each do as collaborative leaders in nonprofit organizations. This book is written for people at all levels and in all institutions who affect how and whether children learn: schools, nonprofits, philanthropies, universities, and families.

Because *relationships* are at the core of collaboration, an easy case can be made that the most important public context for *doing* collaboration is in and around our public schools. PreK–12 education is, for every child, a *place* and a *time* connected by a jumble of *relationships*. Relationships that transform—and are shaped by—pre-existing relationships with parents and family. Relationships that inaugurate, propel, or stymie future relationships with teachers, mentors, and instructional systems. Relationships that introduce, threaten, reward, energize, and elucidate the joys and challenges of friendships. Relationships with collectives—cliques, teams, clubs, and partnerships. Relationships that (at their best) prepare youngsters for their civic duty of improving communities by working well, playing well, and living well with others.

Building relationships between children and the institutions associated with schooling and learning is the most important and overlooked function of formal education. The quality of that relationship—how good each child feels about his or her relationship with the institutions and individuals associated with learning at the preschool and early elementary levels—shapes the educational self-concept, the formation of learning skills, and the educational goals of students. As students progress through the school system, this relationship affects dropout rates, individual career goals, and augurs each young adult's commitment to pursue the further schooling needed to make high career goals realistic.

Building relationships between schools and the public and community institutions that surround them is essential for the effectiveness and continued viability of both schools *and* communities. It is reasonable to expect that the leadership for initiating, building, and maintaining these relationships should come from education professionals. These are the people we trust and train to facilitate our children's growth into learned and learning young adults—but there are also wonderful examples in which this leadership has stepped forward out of political and nonprofit positions.

A common phrase in education literature is "teacher as leader." This book will expand the conventional domain of school leaders (teachers, principals, and others) beyond the four walls of their classrooms or the borders of their school campuses to that of community advocate and coalitional leader. Such leaders build collaborative relationships involving community organizations, social service agencies, government offices, political officials, philanthropies, businesses, parents, other school personnel, and children in order to meet the needs of children and families, serve the schools' instructional agenda, and, in so doing, improve the quality of life for the entire community. Leaders of this type—in schools, nonprofits, and communities—are rare. But we know they're out there . . . and we need more of them.

Teachers, school administrators, volunteers, and nonprofit managers in youth-serving organizations and students preparing for any of these roles will find the discussion and lessons of this book most immediately applicable to their conditions. College deans, university presidents, philanthropists, and government policymakers are in the best positions to carry this discussion forward so as to elevate collaboration as a priority of public leadership, integrate it into the training and certification of institutional leaders, and support the research and development that this emerging field logically deserves.

A Note to Grantmakers

Grantmakers too—in family foundations, corporations, and government agencies—have two overarching reasons for reading this book.

First, your success is as dependent on the vision and follow-through of grant recipients as theirs is dependent on receipt of your grants. Although the relationship of grantmakers and grantseekers is generally viewed as one of inequality, it is in fact hugely interdependent. Progressive and enlightened grantmakers across the nation know that the culture of noblesse oblige is long passed and, in its place, philanthropy's leaders are increasingly skilled collaborators who listen, learn, and shape the world in partnerships with their grantees.

Second, most grantmakers encourage collaboration; many even call for it in their funding guidelines. By strategically reflecting on the stages of building, managing, and evaluating collaboration during your grantmaking decisions, you can improve the transformational impact of your grants. Taking the time to reflect on the reasons, components, stages, skills, and challenges of collaboration will improve your ability to build and support collaborative solutions to the problems you aim to tackle. I encourage you to reflect on how collaboration can help improve the impact of your grantmaking (not in the ideal, but in very specific and measurable ways) and to consider your roles not only as funders of collaborations but also as *partners* whose contributions to your grantees can help leverage effective and accountable collaborative problem solving. Please kick back and enjoy this book. I offer it as a catalyst for reflection.

A Note to the Reader

Can we do this together?

This book continues a dialog that should get each of us thinking about how to expand the scope of our vision, skills, and institutional resources so that building and contributing to successful collaborations become a routine part of how we do business. You and I are collaborators in this conversation!

The words, advice, and teachings of hundreds of colleagues, friends, students, and teachers have shaped the thoughts that fill this book. Don't let the fact that my name appears all by itself on the title page fool you. This work has more authors than I can count! Please join the conversation.

If this book succeeds in generating questions, comments, cases, and suggestions from you and other readers, then we will all benefit from the discussion that results. Not only do I look forward to responding to your communications, but I also promise that subsequent volumes will be stronger and more helpful as a result.

Thanks.
Hank Rubin
hrubin@Collaborative Leaders.org

About the Author

Hank Rubin earned his PhD from Northwestern University, and his MA and BA from the University of Chicago, with coursework at the State University of New York at Geneseo. He grew up in Rochester, N.Y., in the shadow of the work of Saul Alinsky, where he was first exposed to the organizing principle of seeing the world through the eyes of those you wish to lead.

In a career that has spanned the sectors and ranged from national to local in scope—including service in the Ohio Department of Education; the U.S. Department of Health, Education, and Welfare; the Illinois State Board of Education; and the Chicago public schools —Hank Rubin has seen the world through the eyes of a broad cross section of those who affect our national, regional, and local abilities to build the partnerships needed to ensure that all children can succeed.

Rubin entered the 21st century as Ohio's first Associate Superintendent of the Center for Students, Families, and Communities, with state responsibility for special education, early childhood education, gifted education, child nutrition services, safe and drug-free schools, the Ohio Literacy Campaign, and a range of ongoing and new collaborative initiatives including the Ohio Learning First Alliance.

He has taught seventh and eighth grades, run three nonprofit organizations and created several others, directed and taught in the Midwest's largest urban graduate school of Public (government and nonprofit) Administration, served as vice president for sales and marketing in an international manufacturing firm, served as associate vice president for institutional advancement in a large urban university, taught graduate students in education and business management, run for public office, started and managed his own consulting firm, and established the nonprofit Institute for Collaborative Leadership. Rubin has provided counsel and leadership to dozens of collaborative initiatives throughout the United States. He writes and speaks about relationship management with the intellectual clarity of a rigorously trained scholar and the practicality and approachability born of a career path that adheres to the organizing principle that propelled his career from the start (that is, seeing the world through the eyes of those you wish to lead).

Hank Rubin rose to national prominence in the academic study of nonprofit leadership as convener and cochair of the Clarion Initiative (a series of symposia that began at Harvard's Kennedy School and produced a framework for consistent theory and target competencies to guide trainers, educators, and curriculum planners in nonprofit administration). Through his counseling, lectures, and more than 20 publications on topics including school reform, educational goal setting, public ethics, philanthropy, and nonprofit management, Rubin is nationally recognized as an advocate for innovative and collaborative approaches to leadership, training, and public education.

CORWIN
PRESS

The Corwin Press logo—a raven striding across an open book—represents the happy union of courage and learning. We are a professional-level publisher of books and journals for K-12 educators, and we are committed to creating and providing resources that embody these qualities. Corwin's motto is "Success for All Learners."

1

Most of Us Begin by Missing the Point

Cutting Stone

Michelangelo sculpted a series of statues named "The Slaves" in which the torsos of four men appear to emerge from separate rough-hewn blocks of marble. With the smooth, almost warm, flesh of a shoulder here, the turn of a jawline there, a hip stretching into a struggling thigh . . . these sculptures reveal an artist's vision, releasing four figures with chisel and hammer from their stone prisons. Each of us holds the potential of this uncut stone. Anyone who has committed himself or herself to children, families, and some form of public service has within him or her the capacity to be a collaborative leader. This book invites you to look inside yourself and your work—as a person, a professional, and an educator—to find and hone the skills and temperament of collaboration. Trust that they are there. Then, together, let's reflect on and construct a disciplined framework for doing and teaching collaboration and collaborative leadership.

* * *

All but a very small handful of colleges of education miss the point. Scarcely any of the emerging academic programs preparing non-profit administrators have gotten it. But community organizers have almost always practiced it, and children in classrooms since time immemorial could tell when a teacher had it to enlighten their learning.

The rest of us get the point when we see it . . . and feel it even more acutely when it's absent.

"It" is the respect, humility, trustworthiness, interpersonal and organizational skills, credibility, and focused self-discipline that enable a regular person, a teacher, or a public leader to build and sustain the relationships that are necessary to get a job done in public. The public careers of many smart people have risen and fallen on the steep inclines of their superior intellect, oratory, attractiveness, energy, and vision. But without the skills of relationship management (or astute hiring of these skills in a close, supported, and effective adviser), the public profiles of these smart people are unstable or short-lived.

Many people with good intentions and high energy set their hearts on accomplishing a public good of some sort but stumble, ultimately, and throw in the towel. They fail, most often, because they never learned the skills of building the collaborative base of support with workers that is usually necessary to transform dreams into practical and sustainable initiatives. For public leaders and regular people alike, there are few places to turn to acquire the skills of effective collaboration and relationship management. What's missing is a clear and common vision of what it takes to be an effective collaborative leader, and a model, curriculum, or, at least, a series of questions that can be used to begin to understand how to teach someone to be an effective collaborative leader. This book attempts to lay a foundation for the discussion and research that are part of curriculum development.

Why is this important?

Raising Bars

The call to "raise the bar" has become a common theme in the world of public education. Generally, it is used to explain the logic behind the universal campaign for academic standards and standards-based testing. Educators, policymakers, and the general public understand this phrase as a call to expect more of our children and to hold them accountable for meeting our expectations. We all know, of course, that we must increase the resources and expectations of our schools—and school personnel—if we intend to accomplish this. That's why the world of public education is re-examining the rules of teacher certification, tinkering with before- and after-school programming, confronting the instructional implications of school funding, and constantly churning new mixtures of school reform models.

But the transformation of how we do public education is not a challenge to be addressed by educators alone. Schools are owned by their public and that public generally wants to be led (on education matters) by its school leaders. The wonderfully complex relationship of schools, communities, and legislatures creates a hierarchy of educational leaders with *influence* but little *power*. These educators are, in every way, pushing string . . . as you will see in the next chapter. Raising the bar of expectations for these educators will have little impact if we do not, at the same time, improve their collaborative skills so that they can successfully influence the classroom teachers, parents, community leaders, and legislatures who hold the power to influence student achievement.

Here's a short list of what we could not do without collaboration:

- Introduce integrated instruction
- Launch systemic school-based reform (e.g., the type associated with inaugurating instructional programs that support new academic standards)
- Mount a fundraising campaign
- Organize to influence public policy
- Develop and maintain good team teaching
- Coordinate a comprehensive package of family-focused social services
- Link businesses, schools, and community resources in a campaign to reduce gang violence
- Coordinate joint purchasing among school districts

And here's what you can expect when you do collaboration right:

- Everybody in the partnership will be clear regarding the partnership's purpose.
- Everybody in the partnership will be confident that more can be accomplished through the partnership than any one of them could accomplish alone.
- Everybody in the partnership will be looking for ways to align their own work to better contribute to the achievement of the partnership's purpose.
- All key stakeholders (people who have a professional or personal stake in the success of the partnership) will be represented in the partnership.
- All key decision makers (people whose jobs include making decisions that directly impact the purpose of the partnership) will be represented in the partnership.

- One person will be given the resources and authority to manage the logistics of the partnership (e.g., planning agendas, convening meetings, attending to work plans, etc.).
- An action plan will be developed that targets specific products (outcomes) that are aligned with the partnership's purpose and that systemically includes contributions of every partner.
- The partnership will target achievable and ambitious outcomes, beginning with outcomes that will generate early successes (that will strengthen the morale and capacity of the partnership).
- Communication and relationships of people in the partnership will noticeably improve . . . and will yield unexpected and unrelated new accomplishments.
- The partnership will be a place in which people talk about the systemic relationships of all the partners; that is, what and how each partner can contribute to the successes of the whole partnership.

The Importance of Powerlessness

Let's take a short look at the democratic imperative of collaboration.

The problems and needs confronting our schools and communities are far too complex for unilateral, and largely random, action and independent actors, no matter how well-intentioned. It's become cliche to note that it takes a whole village to raise a child; but make no mistake about it, the successful public leaders of the 21st century will be those most skilled at building villages.

Ultimately, democracy demands collaboration. By removing peerage and legalized class differences from civil society, democracy makes each citizen equally powerful—or powerless—in terms of influencing everything from federal laws to local school budgets. To accomplish change in democracy and civil society, the effective leader amasses power—one individual or one institution at a time—until enough has been gathered to crest the barriers and accomplish the goal. In a very real sense, *collaboration is democracy's mandate*.

We tried big government and learned that it can't solve our problems by itself; the private sector shouldn't be expected to; and schools and nonprofits (separately, and in the many combinations we've tried) haven't. If our education and social service problems are to be solved, our arts and culture preserved, our health and quality of life improved, then we must set about building, nurturing, and managing new combinations within our communities—new collaborations.

Not convinced? Then ask yourself, Why do so many schools, nonprofits, and philanthropies fail to have the impact they dreamed of having? It's not for lack of good intentions. Schools and nonprofits attract mission-driven people—intrinsic types who fervently want to make a difference. Nor is it for lack of a good sense of what needs to be done. Schools and nonprofits attract professionals and volunteers who are at least as knowledgeable in their fields as are folks working in business and government agencies.

They fail, in large measure, because getting things done in public *always* entails collaboration, and too many public leaders have never learned how to build, sustain, and direct relationships with the people and organizations with whom they must collaborate.

Collaboration is almost always more time-consuming and challenging than is acting on one's own because collaboration requires skills most of us were never taught, and because a collaborative way of thinking conflicts with the traditional structures and reward systems in which nearly all of us routinely work. So we all have found ourselves trying to avoid collaboration, diminishing its central importance, doing it poorly, or defensively dismissing it as an external mandate—something we do simply because funders and regulatory agencies tell us we must. This is a big mistake.

The Position of Mission

The very structure and purpose of public schools and public service nonprofits demand collaborative skills of their leaders. We are very different from individual entrepreneurs (who can often tuck their chins and plow ahead without regard for collaborative relationships) and corporate moguls (who can build homogenous systems beneath them to accomplish their goals). Nonprofits and public education exist for clear social missions and not for profit, efficiency, or personal gain. Those of us who play a role in leading these organizations become the keepers of these social missions—the advocates and recruiters entrusted to accomplish them. The mandate of public education and nonprofit leaders is to rally resources and communities of support to ensure the achievement of our social missions. *This is a mandate to be collaborative leaders.* And this is what differentiates us— those of us who are effective collaborative leaders—from our corporate and government colleagues.

The social purposes of nonprofit organizations and public education are to change, infuse, or advance knowledge of our ecological, cultural, and individual capacities. These are purposes that transcend the ability of any one person, affect the lives of all people, and demand interpersonal and collaborative skills of those charged with their implementation (practitioners in these two sectors who align the vision and work of others).

There is more that differentiates nonprofits and public schools from the other two sectors:

- Our policy boards are richly diverse collections of agendas and people out of which we must build shared visions, goals, and collaborative teams.
- The constituencies we serve are never homogenous, even though they may share significant characteristics.
- We are increasingly pushed toward interinstitutional collaboration by the growing belief that meeting the education, health care, cultural development, and human service needs of children, families, and communities requires a comprehensive and integrated approach that can be accomplished only through cooperative relationships with other providers.
- The culture of education and nonprofits—along with the comparative limitations of our economic resources—puts pressure on our leaders to recruit and engage volunteers for their minds, talents, and access to resources.
- Our reliance on outside funders necessitates strategic alliances appealing to the institutional self-interests of diverse agencies and donors.
- Our responsibilities to educate the diverse public and offer positive direction to elected policymakers necessitate far-reaching and ever-changing strategic alliances.

The challenge we accept as mission-driven leaders of schools and nonprofits is to become agents of collaboration on behalf of our missions and to develop the collaborative skills that will enable us to achieve them.

2

Pushing String

Several years ago, when I was directing the Public Administration Program at Roosevelt University, I developed the phrase "If you can make a difference, then you have a responsibility to do so." During more than a quarter of a century of work with education and nonprofit organizations, I've grown convinced that this philanthropic temperament is behind nearly every teacher, street corner activist, volunteer board member, literacy tutor, March-of-Dimes canvasser, community organization administrator, school principal, and leader who has ever tried to change a piece of his or her world.

Several years later, as Associate State Superintendent for Students, Families, and Communities in Ohio, I found widespread agreement among professionals at all levels of PreK–12 education when I talked about the educational purpose of all of us who do not deal directly with students in classrooms. Our purpose is not so much to *provide* excellent education for all children as it is to *create tools, partnerships, structures, and opportunities so that every grown-up can find a way to contribute* to providing excellent education for each child in the state.

With all this good intention, why don't we see more good being accomplished and more people involved in doing public good? It's not simply economics that drives the number of available teachers down, creates the growing paucity of qualified candidates in application for district superintendencies, drops the rate of volunteerism and philanthropy in most of our communities, and makes many parents cringe when they hear their youngsters aspire to *making a difference* as opposed to *making a comfortable living*.

Complexity and Cynicism

Americans today share an overwhelming cynicism about public service that can be traced to the gap between good intentions and failed or twisted outcomes. Over 150 years ago, the often-quoted and seldom-read French social observer, Alexis de Tocqueville, raved of the unique emerging character of our then-young nation:

> These Americans are the most peculiar people in the world. You'll not believe it when I tell you how they behave. In a local community in their country a citizen may conceive of some need which is not being met. What does he do? He goes across the street and discusses it with his neighbor. Then what happens? A committee comes into existence and then the committee begins functioning on behalf of that need, and you won't believe this but it's true. All of this is done without reference to any bureaucrat. All of this is done by the private citizens on their own initiative.
>
> Americans of all ages, all conditions, and all dispositions consistently form associations . . . to give entertainments, to found seminaries, to build inns, to construct churches, to diffuse books. (*Democracy in America*, 1862)

Today, there's no simple and direct line connecting the identification of a need, the convening of a committee of peers, and the fulfillment of that need . . . I'm not sure there ever was. Politicians, regulations, daycare problems, second jobs, pervasive apathy, and hundreds of other complicating variables intercede between intentions and outcomes.

Even with technology that allows for instantaneous communication, getting things done in public remains a difficult and complex ambition that relies on one neighbor's fundamental ability to build, nurture, and focus human relationships. In the 1960s and 1970s, we came to call this *organizing*. Our search for understanding led us to learn that organizing entails a body of professional skills and an artistic temperament that was best codified and taught by Saul Alinsky, the father of modern social organizing. Alinsky was a prolific and idiosyncratic writer and trainer whose books and training programs shepherded a generation of labor organizers, civil rights organizers, community organizers, and others onto the streets to change a piece of the world. Alinsky's (1971) *Rules for Radicals* was the blueprint for neighborhood leaders and movement strategists working to mobilize people so as to influence those in power.

In the 1980s and early 1990s, the focus turned to managing schools, social service, arts and culture, health care, economic development, and myriad other nonprofit organizations that existed to accomplish important public missions. It was no longer enough to light passionate fires in the hearts of mission-driven people by organizing them; we demanded that our leaders have the skills to stoke and nurture those fires and focus their heat by managing the organizations that existed to accomplish these public missions. School reform models, Total Quality Management (TQM), Reengineering, and other high-profile management trends (which largely amount to little more than Alinsky's key principles polished to remove their contentiousness and outfitted in suits and ties for corporate consumption) led the nation into an *era of management*. Academicians of a certain stripe throughout the nation struggled to build curricula in nonprofit administration. This effort was spearheaded by prominent sector leaders at Independent Sector, progressive philanthropies such as the Kellogg Foundation, and intellectual enterprises such as the Clarion Initiative (which drew together scores of scholars and practitioners at Harvard's Kennedy School of Government to begin shaping the academic discipline of nonprofit administration). Technical assistance providers such as the Support Centers and Executive Service Corps worked to professionalize nonprofit managers by providing for their training and professional development needs.

Now, in the 21st century, we can expect technology will further shrink our global village. Still, we can't see the future. So, in those private moments of candor, nearly every expert agrees that no one has any idea how technology, demographics, the continued erosion of public confidence in public schooling, and transformative issues such as charter schools and vouchers will change the face of public education *just ten years from now*. Nor can we predict the human and societal implications of welfare reform, global warming, a unified European market and globalized economy, or the extraordinarily complex social challenges that began with the terrorist attacks of September 11. There has been no shortage of public issues around which passionate organizing can occur, yet—until the events of September 11—this has been an era curiously devoid of public passion.

It's not unusual to see families, neighborhoods, and nations rally with dramatic speed and effect against an outside force. Our test as a people, as the smells and memories of terrorism fade, will be whether we have rediscovered our moorings as a nation of activists.

Beyond Toolboxes

In the fields of education, social service, health care, and the arts, collaboration offers the advantage of moving us beyond our *toolbox* mentality: a mentality that has us building the capacities of our organizations in order to accomplish their specific missions by identifying and mastering a prescribed set of tools we think our missions demand. The metaphorical adage, "when your only tool is a hammer, you tend to see all your problems as nails," sheds light on the limitations of this approach. Collaborations not only add tools to the toolbox, they add diversity to the perspectives, broaden our understanding of the problems, and multiply the stakeholders with vested interest in seeing that our mission-driven goals are met.

Collaborations also go a long way toward resolving a common and unattractive characteristic of people in both public and private institutions: the tendency to become so vested in the success of a *single best solution* (ours) or the priority of a *single most important issue* (ours) that we compete in the marketplace rather than looking there to find colleagues who can help us solve the underlying problem. The inherently competitive nature of both the private and public sectors—in which we all see ourselves as battling for a share of the same limited resources—establishes us as competitors with prospective partners. We do battle with them to elevate our competitive positions and, in so doing, disprove their ideas, diminish their importance, and undermine their strivings. This is an inherent inefficiency of the marketplace for which collaborative leaders are the solution.

Collaboration and Competition

Sports provide a powerful metaphor for this solution. It is there that we find some of the nation's best team builders who are motivated by competition. Collaboration and competition go hand in hand. We build teams, partnerships, and cooperatives to get someplace faster, do something better, or make something cheaper. For all but those living alone on desert islands, the construct of collaboration *versus* competition is a false dichotomy. Even the most solitary of individual sports requires deep and sustained partnerships among athletes, coaches, and sponsors in order to succeed. But competition yields the hard statistics and collaboration fills the background. So Americans debate and brag about the stats and ignore the soft art and science of team building. Until we place as much civic value on collaboration as we do on competition (until we teach it in our schools the same way we teach individual academic skills), we will (1) perpetuate the false dichotomy, (2) justify the devaluation of collaboration and civic education as things that children should be taught in school, and (3) continue to produce only those rare few coaches and citizens who really understand how to build collaborative teams.

I've heard educators and community leaders describe collaboration as *herding cats*. Not a bad analogy, but let's take it one step further. In the absence of intentional collaboration, we find ourselves *pushing string* every time we need help in achieving a public goal.

Remember when you and a childhood friend tied string between two tin cans and played "telephone"? When you lifted the can to your ear, you were helpless until your friend lifted the other can to his or her mouth and talked to you. You could have pushed the string joining the two cans toward your partner all day, but you'd have accomplished nothing until he or she chose to lift and stretch the string making it taut, making it work. It was an act of volition . . . a decision to cooperate, an agreement to a shared purpose. Collaboration is not making another person do your bidding: that's co-optation, domination, or authoritarian control. Collaboration is creating a context and decision in which others choose to work with you toward a shared goal.

This new era of collaboration that we are entering is born of the skills of organizing and management. It demands of its practitioners interinstitutional organizing (dependent on the interpersonal skills needed to build and sustain effective relationships) and principled institutional leadership (wherein the principles of sound management are firmly in place before one organizational leader reaches out to partner with another). And because collaborations are the vehicles for those of us who believe *we can make a difference*, this era marks the nexus of pragmatic outcomes-oriented management and public-spirited idealism. Above all else, collaborations exist to accomplish tangible outcomes, changing a little piece of the world with each success.

3

Collaboration and Relationship Management

Who Is a Collaborative Leader?

The moment you decide to contribute to the success of a collaborative enterprise, you may be viewed as a collaborative leader. This concept is quite simple. Once you find yourself in a position to convene a collaboration or to be convened as a partner in another's collaborative initiative, your realm of influence and leadership has expanded to include individuals and institutional representatives in leadership posts within other organizations. This makes you a colleague of these leaders and, prospectively, a leader in your own right. This is true if you are a teacher convening the program directors from the local library and park district to plan an integrated program on astronomy for your seventh graders, a superintendent at the table with the chamber of commerce, or a single mother building a support network of social service providers and GED trainers for a sustained campaign to lift other women in your neighborhood out of the cycle of welfare dependency and into self-confident and permanent employment.[1]

The difference between a *collaborative leader* and a *collaborative partner* is a difference of volition. One chooses to play either a proactive or participatory role in the collaboration. And just as many teachers have mastered the art of teaching from the back of the classroom, one needs to be neither the convener nor a routinely vocal participant during meetings to play a leadership role in strategically moving a collaboration toward its stated mission.

As a rule, only one or two members of a collaboration will take the time to think about how to move the collaboration forward and keep the collaboration alive. This is the central job of the collaborative leader. In this role, we will spend most of our time running the maze of interpersonal and interinstitutional politics that are necessary to build and sustain the interest and involvement of each collaborative partner. Assuming that it is in the interest of the collaboration's mission to engage the full array of partners in the discussion and process of planning and executing the work of the collaboration, this is also the job of the collaborative leader. The effective collaborative leader, therefore, finds a way to help each individual partner understand and sustain a personal connection with the work of the collaboration by attaching that work to each partner's individual or institutional self-interests.

What Distinguishes Collaborative Leaders From Other Types of Leaders?

Collaborative leaders are distinguished by the bridges they build (see Figure 3.1): bridges that individuals willingly cross, connecting (1) their personal needs and motives with a shared public purpose and (2) the work that they do with others whose collaborative alliance can help them do it better, faster, more easily, more enduringly, more efficiently, with bigger impact, with broader ownership, or with higher meaning.

Toward both these ends, one can say that collaborative leaders are interpersonal and interinstitutional relationship managers.

In public, we get things done *with* and *through* people. Effective public leaders don't "lead" as much as they build, sustain, and direct the commitment, skills, and attention of followers and collaborators (just as good teachers do more than "teach," they build and nurture the *relationship* of each child to the resources, skills, and personnel associated with learning and schooling). For collaborative leaders, relationships are the vehicles through which they accomplish the purposes (missions) for which they have developed their skills; *collab-orations are strategic relationships involving individuals and, often, the institutions they represent.*

Figure 3.1   The Bridges That Collaborative Leaders Build

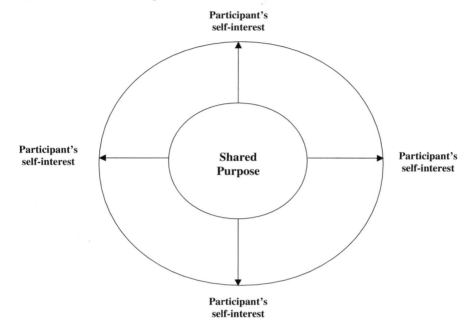

A Word on Institutional Collaboration

When individuals enter into collaborations as representatives of institutions, they are still *individual* collaborators. This is an important point. *Institutions do not collaborate* except *through* individuals and through the formality of contracts and agreements (which, of course, are implemented by individuals). Institutions have neither beating hearts nor collaborative relationships. Therefore, the term "institutional collaboration" is a misnomer.

Individuals who represent institutions in collaborations are challenged to understand and represent (1) the personalities and egos of their institution's leaders and (2) the letter and spirit of the contract or agreement that set the terms for the relationship. Their motivations and decision making inside the collaboration are shaped by self-interests that are influenced by their perceptions of two key drivers: (1) the priorities and personalities of people and (2) the bottom line interests that brought their organization to the table in the first place (see Figure 3.2). Leaders of collaborations involving such representatives are more effective when they understand these tiers of influence.

It's worth repeating that our many levels of interdependence are part of what differentiates the public from the private sector. Unlike

Figure 3.2   What Shapes the Actions of Collaboration's Participants

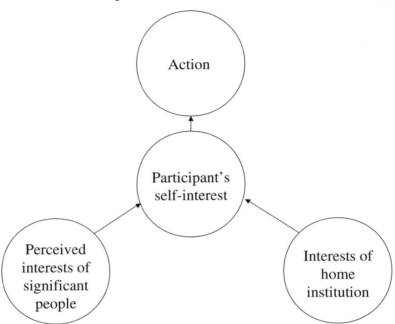

the private sector, those of us in the public sector are mistaken if we believe that we can succeed in some public action by simply attaching our blinders and plowing ahead. Without building and coalescing relationships (partnerships), we will fail to do what's needed in order to achieve our public missions.

Relationships That Bind

Getting things done with and through organizations really means getting things done with and through the people who run the organizations. Convincing leaders to collaborate always reduces to arranging the marriage of individual leaders' self-interests with a shared vision and commitment to act on that vision. Where the leaders go, logic holds, the organizations will follow.

To be effective, we will need to be attentive to this marriage. During the year I helped build the Chicago Panel on Public School Policy and Finance (a coalition of diverse civic organizations convened in the mid-1980s), a bit more than half of my time was spent drafting and refining the coalition's mission and operating procedures to meaningfully support the program goals, mission, and operating practices of the organization of each leader and funder I was recruiting. The rest of my time was spent building relationships of trust and collegiality so that each prospective member and funder could be confident that this initiative would be worth his or her investment.

Similarly, the start-up phase of the Ohio Learning First Alliance (in 2000–2001) entailed arduous months of large and small meetings devoted to identifying a shared vision along with short- and long-term goals toward which each institutional leader was prepared to commit. The work process of developing the vision and goals provided the context for building relationships among leaders that enabled them to overcome their initial cynicism ("What, another coalition?") to enthusiastically launch this new alliance.

Here are some early lessons:

1. Front-end investment in building trusting relationships and shared ownership of the vision is an essential foundation on which to build *sustained* collaboration.

2. Relationships linking institutions succeed only insofar as the structures and procedural practices of the coalition are compatible with those of its member organizations.

3. "Institutional relationships" succeed only insofar as individual relationships are effective.

The ability to build and sustain relationships that bind at both the individual and institutional levels—and the ability to find common self-interests in the diverse missions and goals of independent organizations—defines the effective collaborative public leader.

Working Definitions

The semantical and practical differences between collaboration, co-operation, coordination, alliance, coalition, team, partnership, merger, and the like, are interesting, contentious, worthy of debate, and left to the reader's consideration. In this book, the brick and mortar of our work is fundamentally defined in the following list:

● *Collaboration*: A collaboration is a purposeful relationship in which all parties strategically choose to cooperate in order to accomplish a shared outcome. Because of its voluntary nature, the success of a collaboration depends on one or more collaborative leader's ability to build and maintain these relationships.

- *Collaborative leader*: You are a collaborative leader once you have accepted responsibility for building—or helping to ensure the success of—a heterogeneous team to accomplish a shared purpose. *The ability to convene and sustain relationships influencing individuals and institutions*—and the ability to find and sustain common self-interests in the diverse missions and goals of independent actors—defines the effective collaborative leader.

- *Relationship management*: Relationship management is what a collaborative leader does. It is the purposeful exercise of behavior, communication, and organizational resources to affect the perspective, beliefs, and behaviors of another person (generally a collaborative partner) to influence that person's relationship with you and your collaborative enterprise.

- *Collaborative leadership*: Collaborative leadership is the *skillful and mission-oriented management of relevant relationships*. It is the juncture of *organizing and management*. Whereas community and labor organizers are trained to patiently build their movements through one-on-one conversations with each individual they want to recruit, collaborative leaders do this and more by building *structures* to support and sustain these productive relationships over *time*.

Factors Affecting Collaboration

Time and Formality

In general, the only differences between complex collaborations (that make big demands on their members) and small, focused collaborations (that we easily roll in and out of) are *time* and *formality*.

Within collaborations, formality is a function of time. Let's examine this assertion. Goals that require short, low-maintenance collaborative engagements require few managerial structures and, therefore, can be accomplished with few or no rules and a great deal of informality. Complex goals that can be accomplished only via some sustained operation over time require operating rules, maintenance systems, budgets, and greater formality.

Most collaborative leaders and partners are under pressure to be efficient in the time they spend on collaboration business. Most are so constantly mindful of their institutional and individual self-interests that they want to spend as much time as possible on producing the *outcomes* that the collaboration was convened to accomplish, and *as little as possible on process*. As a result, there is an inherent reluctance to spend time building formal infrastructures, except when the goals of the collaboration could not be accomplished without them.

Itinerant Collaborations

All of us have entered into short-term, or *itinerant*, collaborations in which a number of individuals and institutional representatives convene to tackle specific, clearly defined, and quickly achievable outcomes. We pass in and out of itinerant collaborations just as easily as the tide ebbs and flows; we convene, focus our energies, struggle with obstacles, accomplish our purposes (we hope), and then go our separate ways. When another collaborative need arises, we have a pool of colleagues from which we draw collaborative partners and around whom we build the collaboration. The unique agenda, problem, or need being addressed will define who we optimally want around the table each time we build an itinerant collaboration.

Nonetheless, because we . . .

- Get better at this the more collaborations we build
- Are inclined to look for routines and patterns that will simplify our lives
- Usually find that it is easier to adapt and stretch existing relationships than it is to build new ones

. . . our second, third, and later itinerant collaborations are likely to end up looking like *roundups of the usual suspects*, predictable cliques of individuals and institutional representatives who work well and accomplish goals together. There is nothing wrong with this, if it works. And if it works, then we are on our way to evolving our itinerant collaborations into a long-term *sustained* collaboration.

Sustained Collaborations

These are planned and managed systems of ongoing interaction involving individuals and institutional representatives for whom participation in the collaboration is, essentially, part of their job descriptions. Sustained collaborations are strategic, purposeful, high-maintenance efforts whether they evolve from a series of effective itinerant collaborations or emerge whole cloth as new entities. Their missions are either complex or long term, with flexible goals, and with maintenance costs. As already noted, the fact that sustained collaborations must last a while demands strategic planning, flexibility, and management systems that require formality and structure.

Veracity and Tenacity

There is one more regard in which the issue of *how long a collaboration must last to accomplish its goal(s)* can make a difference. *The longer the spotlight shines on the character of the collaborative leader, the more the success of that collaboration depends on the quality of that character.*

Veracity. An inauthentic collaborative leader, like an unloving lover, may be able to put on a convincing performance for a brief time but will ultimately be brought down by the truth. Countless short-term collaborations have been built to highlight and glorify one organization. Countless have been built so that one "lead organization" could justify its application for funding. But while these activities may portray themselves as collaborations—even succeed in selling themselves as collaborations—they are not collaborations, they are *endorsements*. Weakly skilled collaborative leaders can call in debts and recruit partners from admiring friends, but these collaborations will work only for the short term, until personal and institutional demands draw friends and colleagues away or until they grow tired of the convener's inability to produce anything in the collaboration that fulfills their self-interests.

Tenacity. In the context of collaboration, the key to tenacity is perpetual attention and adaptation to the evolving contexts and self-interests of each collaborative partner. It is the difference between shooting a photograph versus a motion picture, capturing an image in a momentary relationship versus capturing and sustaining a relationship over time.

Conclusion: Collaborative Leaders Succeed With and Through People

Short-term collaborations designed to accomplish some immediate and visible outcome (e.g., to engage the park district and museum in a middle school science curriculum or to influence legislation) are relatively easy to build. They are reactive, time limited, and highly focused. To build this coalition, all one has to do is convince each partner that (1) their individual and institutional self-interests will be served by the coalition and (2) the targeted outcome (instructional program, legislation, etc.) is more likely to be accomplished collaboratively than independently. The value of this collaboration is that it produces a meaningful product, is great practice for building a more complex and sustained collaboration, and strengthens the personal relationships between leaders of collaborating partners. In classic organizing terms, small successes are organizing tools around which collaborative partners can be reconvened and expanded.

In general, the purpose of convening longer-term coalitions is to advance a particular agenda more effectively than individual organizations can do independently. Whether the agenda is meaningful experimentation with varied approaches to education (such as the introduction of systemic school reform strategies), community economic development (such as community development corporations), cultural infusion (such as a museum of art), or something grander yet (such as the United Nations), the challenge is to build both collaborative vision and relationships that are clearly and consistently compatible and important vis-à-vis the evolving missions, practices, self-interests, and leadership of the collaboration's members.

An exercise reportedly used in Saul Alinsky's training program for community organizers puts the virtues of building short-term and long-term alliances in an instructive context. Trainees were asked, "If your goal is to organize a community so that it develops leadership and vision that will enable it to solve its own problems, which of the following problems would you tackle first?"

1. The neighborhood's infestation of rats that are biting and poisoning children on the streets and in their homes

2. The need for a stop sign on a street corner that everyone knows is dangerous, where accidents and near-accidents happen almost daily

The answer is the more immediately achievable and visible accomplishment of getting a stop sign installed. Once the stop sign is erected, it will stand as a source of pride, a symbol of what can be accomplished in coalition, a rallying point for future collaboration . . . a tool that the organizer can use to build the skills, relationships, confidence, and vision needed to attack the more complicated tasks of eradicating rats and leading a community.

* * *

Much of what this book discusses applies to leaders in general. What distinguishes the focus of this discussion is the attention paid to the interpersonal influences and *interinstitutional dimensions* of leadership, the dimensions that reach across the borders of institutions to engage individuals and organizations in collaborative efforts. The focus is on more than just how to get people to want to follow us into battle; it is on the strategies and tools needed (1) to bring diverse individuals and the diverse institutions they represent to a table and then (2) to focus their work on developing the relationships necessary to accomplish a purpose that would otherwise be unattainable by any one of them alone. These are the skills that neighbors need to organize a park cleanup, that social service administrators need to develop new programs with their staff and board members, that teachers need to build a successful dropout prevention program, that cancer society solicitors need to cultivate sustained givers, that religious leaders need to lead and follow their boards of directors, and that parents need to make a difference in their schools and communities—skills that enable activists, community leaders, school administrators, teachers, nonprofit volunteers, arts administrators, and (even) elected officials to do their jobs better.

This is organizing at the interinstitutional level. The building blocks of community and labor organizers are the individual, one-on-one relationships they cultivate. We, as collaborative leaders, build our movements one institutional relationship at a time, with the often-repeated caveat that collaborative relationships happen at both the individual and institutional levels.

* * *

A final note: In the foreword to my book *Collaboration Skills for Educators and Nonprofit Leaders*, U.S. Congressman Danny K. Davis wrote, "Lord knows, we need to understand, learn, and teach young and aspiring public leaders how to build and manage their relationships with other public leaders." These basic skills are essential in every sector, they do not vary—in any principled way—across the sectors, and they will define—in the end—whether or not we succeed in our civic mission of building communities that raise successful families and children.

Note

1. Note that collaborative leaders live in the village (either the physical or professional community) they are trying to build. It is not unusual for outside experts to be brought on in order to bridge differences, help strategize operations, or facilitate the group's process; but these outsiders are *collaborative facilitators*, not collaborative leaders.

4

Educators as Collaborative Leaders

Why Public Education?

Our nation is a constitutional republic predicated on principles of democracy, born in the blood of civil action, founded by advocates of equality, liberty, and human dignity. Nowhere does our Constitution mention (let alone call for) the free market economy that has emerged as the domestic and international hallmark of our nation. Nonetheless, in our coffee shops and bars, Americans express more confidence in the fairness of the free market's ability to distribute resources than in our constitutionally prescribed government's ability to do this. Collectively, Americans have lost a shared consciousness of democratic principles and have elevated free market principles as the framework for shaping our national priorities and policies on domestic welfare and international relations. We have always expected the burden of building a shared public consciousness to rest in our schools.

* * *

Ask an average American, "What is the purpose of public education?" and you are apt to hear, "To prepare students to get and hold decent jobs." Ask a more reflective neighbor, "What is the purpose of public education?" and you may hear, "To enable each child to discover and develop his or her full potential." But only an excruciatingly small proportion of Americans, when asked the same question, will harken back to the visions of John Dewey and Horace Mann—two of the philosophical architects of American public education—and answer, "To preserve democracy and enable each child to develop as an individual and as a contributing member of the community, economy, and society." John Dewey told us, "Democracy has to be born anew every generation, and education is its midwife."

From the start—in the colonies' little red schoolhouses—schools were places where education happened to prepare each child (at least each male child) to be a wage earner and a good citizen. We've never lost sight of these individual and collective (academic and civic) purposes of public education, although the relative value placed on each purpose has changed dramatically over time.

Today some would contend that the standards movement and the tight economy are not conducive to public education's civic mission, the former placing the priority on skill building and the latter on reducing resources available for undervalued civic outcomes. Academic content standards are predicated on the foundational skills of reading and mathematics. Character education, values education, service learning, and the like are easy first-round budget cuts when districts and states have to tighten their education belts. In essence, this argument amounts to pitting the individual and collective purposes of public education against each other. This is an intellectually fatuous and socially dangerous position to be in. We have no more right to waste and frustrate a child's life—by instilling a committed sense of social responsibility and failing to convey to that child tools and skills for survival and professional achievement—than we do to create the public danger of developing professionally competent people who have no sense of social purpose or responsibility.

Certainly schools and homes share the responsibility for developing both the private and public child. But schools are the places where professionals are consistently brought to attend to each individual's skills and where community is created to develop the social self. Schools are the four walls in which the challenge of this dichotomy is confronted every day.

The Case for Teachers as Collaborative Leaders

Creating a Learning Environment, One Relationship at a Time

In the cool objectivity of reflection, was your formal education a good experience? Chances are, all else being equal, if your answer is yes you've gone on to pursue the educational credentials necessary for the career you've dreamed of or the job you realistically expect to achieve, and you owe a big "thank-you" to one or more of your teachers. If your answer is no, in all probability, you're stuck without the educational qualifications you think are necessary for the job you want to be in, and you never had a teacher who helped you understand that achieving your dreams relies on the height and persistence of your ambition to learn.

Whether you are rich or poor, your perception of the quality of your prior school experience—how good you feel about the quality, relevance, and rewards of the schooling you received—may be the best predictor of whether you *choose* to continue your education and certainly is the best predictor of whether you *desire* to continue your education.

With computers in preschools; impersonal and decaying large urban school districts straddling politics, financial ruin, low test scores, and high dropout rates; the escalating battle between schools and the streets (or the malls) for control of the educational agenda for our children; and the easy isolation offered by television and video games that mollify and transport youngsters away from learning relationships, the human truth of formal education remains. Much like eating clams or holding hands, if you feel rewarded by what came before, you are more likely to choose to do it some more.

This is the fundamental behavioral truth of relationship building. We are drawn to, and return to, that which is rewarding. All these years, we have been concentrating on reading, writing, and arithmetic (and more progressively on logic, literary awareness, and creativity) as the essential products of elementary and secondary education. But while these are important outcomes of public schooling, they are the *primary* outcomes only for those consumers (students) who choose to stop their education at or before high school graduation.

For everyone else, these studies are the elemental and essential *tools of the trade*—the things that teachers do with us and to us as we work together to shape a sense of our capabilities, self-worth, and prospective future in education. These studies are our individual primers, intended to be the first things—not the last things—we set out to learn.

The purpose of good education is not only to teach us the primers but also to teach us how to learn them . . . and to want to learn more. When education succeeds in this way for a student, it's almost always due, in large part, to a teacher who made the connection work.

Here is the concept I want to drive home: The focus of the good teacher is on process as much as on content. All grown-ups remember the quality of their relationships with the tones and attitudes of their favorite teacher(s) much more than the topics the teacher(s) covered in class. We remember how these teachers made us feel about ourselves within the learning environment. These teachers were collaborative leaders who drew students into a shared vision of learning as a rewarding lifelong effort—a loftier and longer-term goal than that of most collaborative leaders.

These teachers—of yesterday and today—are radical educators for whom the goal is lifelong learning, not simply instruction. They never close their classroom doors to teach in private. Their classrooms are not their domains; rather, they are their springboards. They convey to their students skills and resources and a lifelong commitment to connect them to practical experiences in new and creative ways. This attention to connecting the individual learner in a sustained, child-centered relationship with diverse learning resources is at the core of contemporary models of special education and gifted education. It's how school psychologists and school librarians do business. It's inherent in the leadership roles that we ask Safe and Drug-Free School Coordinators and the emerging variations of specialized literacy coordinators to play. (To make writing and reading this book a bit easier, I'll call all these educators "teachers.")

Teachers, as the primary agents of education, play the largest role in shaping and controlling the effectiveness of students' relationships with their learning environments and the process of learning. Good teachers translate the complex and often competing demands we place on them into individual strategies for connecting learners to learning. You will find many of these same demands (and strategies) at work in the United Nations, at labor/management bargaining tables, at condominium board meetings, and in economic development commissions.

We expect these relationships to be productive in the eyes of all the parties involved. We expect them to be measurably related to a meaningfully larger purpose. We expect the time we spend together to be well planned, pleasurable (at least bearable in proportion to the benefit we derive), and efficiently productive. We expect all parties to make their best contributions to the success of the relationship.

These expectations are the sum and substance of *relationship management*: the art and science of building and sustaining the relationships necessary to get things done. For a good teacher, relationship management entails building, nurturing, and instilling a relationship between each student and his or her education—a relationship that is viewed by each student as pleasurable, important, challenging, and meaningful.

For children growing up in poverty, the role of teachers in shaping educational self-worth is especially important because, to these children, teachers may be the only flesh-and-blood purveyors of school-like education and models of educational achievement. They are the truth-telling evaluators of educational "fit" (both judging and influencing whether students find comfort, fulfillment, and the tools to succeed in an educational environment). For these children, teachers, especially early elementary teachers, have been found to play an even larger role than mothers in influencing long-term educational aspirations.[1]

In a world of international trade and competition, the effectiveness of our teachers as collaborative leaders takes on national importance. *There can be no more important education or economic priority for this country than to keep our children going to school for as long as it takes them to learn what they need to learn to acquire the credentials that will give them a realistic shot at the professional goals they will set for themselves.* (Take a breath and read that sentence again!) Short of chaining our children to their desks, the only way we will make this happen is by increasing their *desire* to complete their secondary schooling and pursue postsecondary education. We count on teachers to build the relationships that instill this desire. In this very real way, teachers guard the gates of tomorrow's national security.

Congressman Danny Davis's foreword to *Collaboration Skills for Educators and Nonprofit Leaders* (Rubin, 1998) further cautioned us,

> Nobody trying to get something done in the public sector can succeed by him or herself. Whether you are a teacher, superintendent, community activist, nonprofit leader, economic development administrator, philanthropic board member, or congressman, the fact is, if you don't know how to build effective and ongoing collaborative relationships with other people, you won't succeed.

This is the *fourth* "R" all children need to learn to grow up to be competent adults: Reading, 'Riting, 'Rithmatic, and *Relationship building and management.*

As America's corporate sector settles into its age of managerial enlightenment (learning, at last, through TQM, reengineering, and the like, that businesses succeed as much through relationships as through growth models and robotic production lines), the new goal of every sales, marketing, and customer service department is to build relationships of trust and loyalty with their customers. In such relationships, the needs of each customer are so well projected and fulfilled, and buying from the company is so comfortable and rewarding, that every customer will desire to do it again—regardless of the product's price. Similarly, students who find education comfortable and appropriately rewarding are bound to want (and more likely to pursue) more education, no matter how difficult they may find their schoolwork to be. Students (first) and their families (second) are the most important client–partners of our public education systems. Their relationships with our schools will not be strengthened by reduced expectations, comfortable fluff, or classroom candy. They will be strengthened when we shift the way we institutionally relate to them from a *parental model* to an *enlightened consumer model*—an approach to public education that treats students and their families as collaborative partners in mutually productive relationships.[2]

The question is, How do we increase the desire of our consumers —our students—to seek continued education? The answers lie, in part, in (1) the demanding challenge of restructuring early education to lay the groundwork for these relationships right off the bat and (2) developing training, incentives, and accountability for all educators to raise the priority of relationship management at all levels of education and for all of schooling's constituencies.

This will demand no less than a reconsideration of, first, how our colleges of education prepare our future educators and, second, the priorities that we as a nation set for funding and evaluating elementary and secondary education. Each factor will influence the success of the other.

As educators in a nation caught up in the momentum of the standards movement, we must encourage a balanced focus on both the academic content of what we teach and the social and civic skills that children learn. Relationship management should be a priority—at the center of how we recruit, prepare, and certify educators. And it should shape what we expect of—and how we measure the effectiveness of—our teachers and school administrators. How we prepare and evaluate them and the status we afford them should be centered on their ability to develop and nurture, one at a time, the relationships that will ensure a generation of committed learners.

A Teacher's Review

Collaborative leaders are interpersonal and interinstitutional relationship managers. Isn't it time we thought of elementary and secondary teachers in this capacity? Educators in the 21st century need to be skilled, creative, and collaborative community leaders on behalf of the learning needs of children and their families. This is a larger role than is conventionally implied by the phrase "teachers as leaders" and pertains to more than the centrally important relationships that teachers will develop and manage with the students in their charge.

Teachers in the 21st century will be village builders. Through conventional and computer-assisted means, they will connect with a universe of people and resources. They will convene the social service providers whose services will help to ensure that students can learn and families can promote students' learning. They will build relationships with corporations, philanthropists, and government agencies that will augment their limited resources so that children can succeed. They will develop partnerships with other public institutions such as libraries, parks, and police districts and with private interests such as chambers of commerce and local banks so that services and programs can be coordinated and communities can be organized to support specific developmental needs of children and their families. They will do all this or we will never achieve the academic and civic purposes of public education.

Teaching Collaboration for Teaching's Public Purpose

Let's take a look at the other purpose of teaching and public education.

The greatest challenge of teaching is the stark dichotomy of its functions. On the one hand, we expect teachers to define the capacity of each individual child and, through the magic of effective teaching, to open each child's eyes to that capacity, align instruction, develop skills, and enable each child to cultivate that capacity so as to reap its rewards. On the other hand, we call on teachers to be John Dewey's midwives of American democracy, infusing social and civic skills in the education and worldviews of their students . . . preparing young people to be effective citizens and adults. Teachers need skills of collaborative leadership to accomplish this civic purpose.

We know that children learn best not merely by "doing" but by doing with others—by engaging in learning activities with other youngsters to learn not only the substance of their lessons but also the skills of building and managing the relationships that will be necessary for learning and applying knowledge throughout their lives. The capacity to forge and nurture effective relationships influences not only what and how much we can learn but also what we can do with that knowledge once we acquire it. Relationship-building and relationship-management skills will be at least as important in the lives of our children as their math, science, and reading skills . . . but where in the elementary, secondary, and collegiate curricula of our schools—when in the lives of our children—is formal attention paid by any caring adult to teaching children how to collaborate?

The answer may be preschool and kindergarten. These are the years that focus on social—not academic—learning. But once we get into the academic years, students are rarely exposed to instructional time, applied reflection, or expository exercises on the skills of building and managing effective collaborative relationships. This is a portentous gap in public education. There is no other set of principles or skills that we all acknowledge to be essential yet teach (if at all) in such a haphazard fashion.

Service learning and character education are the closest we come in the academic years of public education to reflective instruction addressing the developmental skills of building and sustaining relationships for personal and public productivity. But even here, the teaching of collaborative skills is almost always inferential. As educators, we send youngsters out on public service field trips to explore and experiment . . . to intern at the knees of practitioners and learn what can be learned through observation and personal reflection. And when we regroup after these explorations, we are nearly never deliberative in addressing the particular skill set of collaboration with students. Each of us in education would be sorely challenged to find lesson plans, teaching materials, and assessment tools aimed at helping students to develop their collaboration skills. This is where the teaching of nonprofit administration was in the 1970s and early 1980s—viewed as an art form, learned by observing and working in the presence of skilled mentors, learned best by those who were artistically inclined (predisposed to learning this particular art form), and devoid of a coherent instructional framework that enabled everyone to learn.

We don't send children into a library expecting them to learn to read. We first give them some basic skills so that they may be comfortable and effective when they get there, and we motivate them with a vision of the doors that libraries, books, and reading can open.

Similarly, we can't expect to send children and young adults in programs of service learning (whether in elementary schools or universities) out into communities to do service internships without first conveying to them some basic skills to help them interpret and succeed in the collaborative work of public service. But we send them out to sink or swim with, perhaps, some preliminary substantive training (to acquaint them with the content of the work) but not the skills of working in teams, building consensus, designing structures that support collaborative decision making, and the like. We expect them to learn these skills on the job. This metaphor goes one step further. Just as we can't expect children to have successful library experiences if we do not adequately prepare them, there is no reason to believe that any child will voluntarily seek a library experience without such preliminary training. Basic collaboration skills, therefore, are essential not only for making service learning work but also for making it meaningful.

Our aim, therefore, should be

- To persuade faculty and deans in colleges of education to introduce the competencies of collaboration and relationship management in the required coursework of teacher education programs
- To persuade parents, teachers, superintendents, and school board members that collaboration and relationship-management skills are teachable and learnable priorities for their instructional programs

The Easy Case for Principals and Superintendents as Collaborative Leaders

We don't need to break through as many preconceptions and stereotypes to agree that we expect principals and superintendents to be leaders. We know that we need our educational administrators to understand their role and function effectively as educational leaders. Effective educational leaders are not simply school administrators (site-based managers and regulators); educational leaders are community-wide advocates, mentors, and conveners.

Education is a process toward which we all must contribute. *Schools are buildings*, simply places where the process of education occurs.

This is an important distinction that Paul Houston, executive director of the American Association of School Administrators, makes very well. The effective leaders of the 21st century will be *super-intendents of education*, not *superintendents of schools*. They will be community leaders operating on behalf of the instructional and learning needs of children and their families. They will rally the resources, prick the consciences, and focus the energy of individuals and institutions from every sector of their communities so as to educate their children. They will be boundary-spanning advocates and administrators for whom "the schools" will be only one locus of their work. They will be measured far less by the effectiveness and efficiency of the administration of their buildings and staffs and far more by their ability to rally and sustain the devoted attention and resources of their entire community in relationships that meaningfully enhance the educational achievements of their students (perhaps reflected, one day, by the things those students accomplish long after they have left formal education). The same will be expected of principals.[3]

They will be collaborative leaders. Follow the workday schedule of superintendents and principals today, and you will find that many already are. Follow the schedule of superintendents and principals in districts with full-service schools and you will find administrators who have made collaborative community leadership the central theme of their professional lives.

Superintendents and principals have three influential constituencies: their school boards or local school councils, their teaching and nonteaching staffs, and the individuals and institutions in their communities. Superintendents and principals are the conduits, catalysts, and executors for ensuring that *education reflects the will of the board, the skill of the teachers, and the best investment of the entire community*. This challenge, which is almost never without conflicting self-interests between competing constituencies, is the most compelling collaborational responsibility of educational leaders.

In their larger context, the universe of prospective collaborative partners for principals and superintendents includes individuals and administrative units on their staffs as well as individuals and institutions from across their districts, from other parts of their states, and in model districts and professional associations throughout the nation. Their role, as collaborative leaders, involves convening—and supporting the convening by others—of the variety of individual and institutional resources that will collaborate to accomplish targeted objectives that will improve educational outcomes.

Facilities planning, full-service schools, extended school year, and before- and after-school programming are all best done through deliberative and sustained collaborations.

Superintendents and principals have the same collaborative leadership responsibilities that the first section of this chapter spells out for all educators . . . but in addition to having a larger territory, they also have the generic and routine collaborative responsibilities associated with their school boards, staffs, and communities. I contend that educators share the responsibility of helping every grown-up in the community find the best way to partner for children's learning success. The added burden for school administrators in this regard is the collaborative responsibility of creating an environment within their schools and districts that supports and encourages every educator to provide this collaborative leadership.

* * *

The rest of this book focuses on the concept of relationship management and the skills and principles of effective collaborative leadership. More than for any other constituency, this is a book for teachers, other student service personnel, principals, superintendents, the sphere of nonprofit and community leaders whose missions and work revolve around building villages of support to raise capable and happy children, and the thought leaders who shape curriculum and instruction in our colleges of education.

Notes

1. Slaughter-Defoe, D. T., & Rubin, H. (2001). A longitudinal case study of Head Start-eligible children: Implications for urban education. *Educational Psychologist, 36*(1), 31–44.

2. In May 2000, the National Council for Accreditation of Teacher Education (NCATE) approved dramatically new criteria evaluating the preparation of teachers and school administrators. Among the changes is compelling emphasis on *partnerships* between college personnel and field-based practitioners in the preparation, delivery, and evaluation of collegiate programs. ("Professional standards for the accreditation of schools, colleges, and departments of education: 2002 edition." NCATE, Washington, DC.)

3. The most dramatic change introduced by the new NCATE standards is the performance-based, results-driven expectation that effective preparation of education's professionals is best measured by improvement in PreK-12 students' performance.

5

Constructing Models

It's all in your head!

Whether you choose to act collaboratively—and whether you act collaboratively well—depends on whether you understand collaborative action as a meaningful and personally practical way to get something done.

Collaboration cannot be a burden—a troublesome, overlaying set of duties and work that must be done *in addition* to the normal work we do. Instead, it needs to be a comfortably adapted way to get our work done, steps we take to produce a product that adds value to our efforts.

Collaborative action needs to have a simple and easily communicated purpose, and its process must be clear, productive, and replicable. (And because it needs to be data driven, this book is ultimately a dissertation of theories—supported by logic, anecdotal data, and years of field and classroom experience—but theories, nonetheless, that need to be explored and tested.)

In the remaining chapters we will develop several models, frameworks, and symbols designed to begin clarifying the purpose and process of collaboration.

* * *

The Purpose of Collaboration

Collaboration is a means of aligning people's actions to get something done. When used to construct itinerant or short-term alliances, it is the tool of the problem solver. When used to build sustained or long-term alliances, it is the tool of the change agent. In either case, when collaborations succeed in causing change, they are the tools of systems thinkers who recognize that *changing systems means changing people . . . and that influencing change in other people only occurs by managing our relationships with them.*

Systems thinkers look at forces and institutional structures, assets, and barriers. Their work is to align assets to achieve goals and overcome barriers. They combine the strategies of "Quality" management and "asset-based" organizing. A *collaborative* systems thinker further combines these qualities with a skill set that engages human partners in aligning systems and assets to do good work *on purpose*!

Turning Arrows

Most systems are not aligned. More times than not, individuals, the programs they run, the offices they work in, and the institutions they create are pointed like random arrows in widely varied directions, aimed at visions and goals that aren't aligned. This is as frustrating for administrators as it is for the overwhelming numbers of committed and hardworking people toiling toward unaligned random outcomes.

Even when we introduce a shared institutional purpose, the momentum of ego, politics, funding patterns, professional practice, regulations, and the like keeps arrows from turning toward the shared purpose.

Systems thinkers are attentive to turning these arrows toward a shared purpose until efficiency, effectiveness, and geometry of alignment eventually take shape.

The What

During the past two decades, the Quality movement has emerged to give voice and empirical grounding to the compelling logic of systems thinking. A variety of Quality-management frameworks has surfaced—including TQM, TQE, reengineering, Malcolm Baldrige, and the like—to answer the question, *What* must be aligned if we are to effectively and efficiently focus the resources of a system on getting a targeted job done?

Baldrige offers perhaps the most rigorously tested list of concrete components of systems thinking and is the most popular contemporary management system to make the crossover from corporate to educational leadership. It is a respected business practice with a growing following in public education. To *do* Baldrige right, practitioners must address at least the following:

- Leadership
- Strategic planning
- Stakeholder focus
- Fact-based decision making
- Outcome orientation (continuous improvement)
- Sensitivity to human resources
- Management systems

These are the parts of systems that Baldrige tells us must be aligned. Practitioners are challenged to make these topics (and comparable frameworks in other Quality systems) the prism through which they view the functions of systems and the roles people play in them. In this book, we will tweak and adopt these Baldrige principles as our lexicon for systems thinking.

Two key contributions of the Quality movement are (1) the deconstruction of "the system" into parts and levers (these seven principles) and (2) the introduction of procedures, which, if followed, align the parts toward a common vision and reconstruct the system to sustain that alignment. In effect, it gives us the game board, pieces, and rules so that we know *what* must be done to change and move systems. Relationship management focuses on inspiring, engaging, and sustaining the individuals who will play; collaboration answers the *how*.[1]

In the absence of formal attention to making these personal connections, the Quality movement has had some high-profile examples of forced alignment, such as people being driven to align their work with data, benchmarks, best practices, continuous improvement, and the like more out of fear of reprisals than because of collaborative commitment. I saw this type of implementation of system alignment in the Chicago offices of the U.S. Postal Service during the 1990s. Important key indicators were met and structural improvements were put in place within a system that was marked by fear, anxiety, anger, high turnover at all levels except the very top, and a kick-the-dog syndrome that all but justified the politically incorrect phrase "going postal." Predictably, when force is used to implement change, only *structural* change will persist when that force is removed. The human contributions to change (e.g., culture, climate, how people deal with each other, the energy people bring to their work) will revert to their prechange status when coercion is removed. In the workplace, collaboration is a tool for developing a shared sense of responsibility and investment in decisions and actions so that change is owned by the workers long after top leadership has moved on.

Fortunately, examples of this nature are few and far between. But the Quality movement continues to be more focused on the game board, pieces, and rules than on forging connections with the people who must play the game. The remaining chapters of this book contribute to system alignment by explicitly addressing the human context, tools, and skills that answer the question, *How* do we develop collaborative partnerships toward shared goals?

The Why

Why do we bother? Some view collaboration as a meaningful end in and of itself. The 1960s were famous for celebrating the belief that we can solve big social problems by sitting together and talking. We will have evolved only slightly if we believe today that we can solve those same problems by simply working and playing well together. Collaboration is more than a better set of rules for sandbox play. Collaboration is a means to an end . . . and that end is the clear and transcendent goal or purpose that caused us to collaborate in the first place.

In Ohio, that end was *partnering for student success*. Student success was defined as performance on new achievement tests attached to new academic standards. We built new collaborative partnerships to help implement the new academic standards. Our mantra, our purpose, and our *why* were clear—to raise the bar of expectations for student achievement, close the gap between low-achieving and high-achieving districts (and between each individual student's academic performance and academic capacity), and find new and effective ways to engage more grown-ups in partnerships that support improved student achievement.

A Quality framework for our efforts in Ohio might have looked like the chart shown in Table 5.1. For each goal, the chart asks us to consider the role, contribution, and action to be taken to ensure a systemic approach, according to a Quality perspective.

Table 5.1 A Framework for System Alignment
[The Ohio Example of Why and What]

Why? [Our shared goals]	What? [Quality principles of system alignment]
Raise Expectations	Leadership
	Strategic Planning
	Stakeholder Focus
	Fact-Based Decision Making
	Sensitivity to Human Resources
	Management Systems
	Continuous Improvement
Close the Gaps	Leadership
	Strategic Planning
	Stakeholder Focus
	Fact-Based Decision Making
	Sensitivity to Human Resources
	Management Systems
	Continuous Improvement
Partner for Student Success	Leadership
	Strategic Planning
	Stakeholder Focus
	Fact-Based Decision Making
	Sensitivity to Human Resources
	Management Systems
	Continuous Improvement

The How

Having looked at *why* and *what*, let's remind ourselves that collaboration is the categorical answer to "How." *How* do we align systems through Quality practices to accomplish our goals? In education and all other portions of the public sector, we do it with and through our relationships with people. *Collaborative leaders are distinguished as systems thinkers who understand that systems are nothing more than mental constructs that improve our effectiveness as relationship managers. We move systems only by moving the people who comprise them.*

Tyrants bend systems, forcing people to follow. Collaborative leaders align the will and the work of people, causing systems to follow.

Note

1. The Quality movement does not ignore the How. Edward Deming, a self-professed follower of John Dewey, recognized that *all change is personal* and guided the Quality movement toward an integration of systems and personal change. However, emerging as it has from the physical sciences (Baldrige practices were orginally designed by chemists), the technology and language of Quality associated with the What (the movement of systems and their parts) is more broadly known, more advanced, and more generally associated with implementation of Quality systems than are the Deming values associated with personal and individual change (the How).

6

Collaboration's Life Cycle

Overview

There is a genius to the simple and practical 12-step systems that have become the hallmark of self-help traditions and personal empowerment programs. Such systems stretch our thinking to the limits of what our minds can realistically hold onto at any given moment, and they give us a protocol for ordering our action and planning. There is good precedent for twelve, it seems to work . . . so let's use it! The 12 phases of collaboration's life cycle sketched out on the next few pages give us a lens through which to look at both the substance and process of collaboration. With this tool we can

- Look at just what it takes to do collaboration[1]
- Develop a checklist that we can begin to use to assess the status, strengths, needs, next steps, and timelines of collaborations that we observe and/or join

The 12 Phases of Collaboration's Life Cycle

During the critical first steps of collaboration's life cycle, the most fundamental questions are asked and answered by the individual or small group intent on launching the initiative. Many initiatives never make it past Phase 1 to become collaborations. (Undoubtedly, many that do never should.) Phases 2, 3, and 4 are the points at which key steps are taken to address the who and how of recruiting partners. Phases 5, 6, and 7 focus on the collaboration's leadership and planning. Phases 8, 9, and 10 are devoted to the quality and strength of bonds connecting partners to and within the collaboration. And Phases 11 and 12 address the disciplined steps of accountability and renewal.

Phase 1: Why Collaborate?

What do you really want to achieve? Has the problem(s) you wish to solve or the vision you hope to accomplish been reduced to its most potent lever: the action or achievement that will have the greatest impact on your goals? *Is the goal best achieved through collaboration?* Have you carefully considered the questions of how and why a collaborative approach improves the likelihood of accomplishing your goals?

Phase 2: Outcomes? Decision Makers?

What are the targeted outcomes? Who are the essential decision makers? Did you take the time to refine your thinking about the general goal(s) considered in Phase 1 so that the outcomes you hope to target are clear enough to make it possible for you to identify *by name* the decision makers who control or influence your ability to succeed (who themselves must be influenced to accomplish the desired outcomes)? Did you stop to consider the desirability and likelihood of recruiting these named decision makers into your collaboration before making contact? When decision makers *who were not likely to participate* were selected, did you identify alternatives, such as individuals who (1) directly influence these decision makers, (2) are themselves desirable members of the coalition, and (3) are likely to respond favorably to recruitment?

Phase 3: Stakeholders?

Who are the stakeholders who need to be involved? Did you identify *by name* the full range of essential stakeholders, individuals, and organizations with knowledge, history, celebrity, credibility, influence, or resources, or who otherwise have a stake in the outcome(s) you are targeting? Are these resources represented among the assets of your stakeholders? Did you consider all the players who have capacity to influence whether your outcome can be achieved and weigh the pros and cons of involving each? Did you assess the resources (human, material, informational, and financial) you may need to accomplish your outcome(s)? Did you assess the desirability and likelihood of recruiting each of these named stakeholders before making contact? When you identified an individual *within a desired organization* who proved to be either not suitable or recruitable, did you then identify another prospect within that organization who is both suitable and recruitable?

Phase 4: Frame and Recruit

Did you develop a unique and tailored strategy to recruit each prospective partner? Did your preplanning include consideration of who—from the perspective of each prospective partner—should make the overture and what—from the perspective of each prospective partner—will satisfy the prospect's self-interests and enthuse him or her about participating in your collaboration? It's worth noting, at this step, that *attendance* and *participation* are not synonymous. Particularly at these early phases, individual partners may choose to attend meetings out of curiosity and not out of commitment. **Has care been taken to sustain an attitude of recruitment during the early phases of the collaboration?** Has attention been paid to engage each partner in (a) discussing and reaching at least some general agreement on the mission and goals of the collaboration and (b) solidifying the connection of each partner's self-interests with the emerging mission and operation of the collaboration?

Phase 5: Leaders, Structure, Roles, and Rules

In building the collaboration, did you address the key functions of collaborative leadership outlined in Chapter 7? In itinerant collaborations, these functions may be informally assumed and shared by partners during the brief duration of the initiative. In sustained collaborations, has attention been paid to ensure adequate levels of continuity, responsibility, and accountability for fulfilling the most important of the functions introduced in Chapter 7? **In sustained collaborations, has there been reflection on the question of whether formalization of leadership, structure, functional roles, and operating rules would help or hurt the collaborative process?** Has the collaboration strategically moved toward formality, *with attention paid to* *ensure* that all partners are comfortable and invested in the structure, leadership, roles, and rules? Or did the collaboration move too abruptly or prematurely, scaring away some partners who have attended and could contribute to the collaboration but who may not have felt adequately connected to the collaboration or supported by their organizations to formally commit in this fashion? Were routine meeting dates established for the collaboration (and, if relevant, for its parts)? Have routine communications been developed and deployed to keep all essential players informed of the coalition's work? If need be, has the collaboration's convening leadership been available to stay on in the role of administrative leadership until the group's cohesion and its members' commitment were strong enough to support the move to formal decisions?

Phase 6: Develop an Action Plan

Did the collaboration develop strategic plans with benchmarks so that all its members know where the collaboration is going and can measure where it's been? Have the plans (or their summaries) been circulated, reviewed, and endorsed by all partners and their institutions at strategic times? **Have partners been encouraged to discuss the collaboration's action plan in terms of how specific portions connect to the institutional missions and self-interests that they represent?**

Phase 7: Begin With Successes

Did the collaboration begin with short-term plans that targeted successes around either its most urgent or least controversial goal(s)? Has the collaboration's action plan been built on this (these) early success(es)? How has the collaboration leveraged early successes as a tool for organizing, focusing, encouraging, and leading? (E.g., Have these early successes become part of the folklore? Are they routinely referred to in publications?)

Phase 8: Build Bonds Between Partners

How has the collaboration paid attention to building the essential bonds between collaborative partners? Has an internal environment of trust, loyalty, and high professionalism been created early on so that later on, partners are willing to make the compromises that will certainly be demanded in the context of collaborative decision making?

Phase 9: Celebrate Successes

What has been done to make sure that collaborative partners—both individual representatives and lead decision makers in the institutions they represent—feel good about their continued participation in the collaboration? Has the collaboration celebrated its successes with internal recognitions to strengthen these bonds? Has external publicity been used as a tool to build momentum, support, and pride among partners and key external constituencies?

Phase 10: Assess, Adjust, Reinforce Bonds

Do leaders really know if individual partners feel well connected to and supportive of the collaboration? What tactics have been used —one on one or in the whole group—to make sure that this connection is considered and attended to? How does this collaboration routinely measure, adjust, and reinforce the bonds between collaborative partners in the collaboration?

Phase 11: Goal-Centered Accountability

How does the collaboration measure its progress? Does it have clear indicators of success? Are these indicators known to all members of the collaboration? Are they connected to its goal(s)? Are they reviewed and updated routinely? Are they owned by the partners and partner institutions? **How does what is measured relate to what is done?** Are systems of accountability created and connected to these goals? Do partners understand and talk about their goal-centered accountability?

Phase 12: Revisit and Renew Mission

Are the collaboration's partners aware and routinely reminded of the mission and goals of the collaboration? Does the collaboration stop to revisit its mission, especially at significant benchmarks or when there are changes in external conditions? Is the collaboration flexible enough to explore the pros and cons of all possible options, including (1) modifying the mission and/or operating ground rules, (2) retaining them intact, (3) expanding or redirecting the mission, (4) taking a vacation, or (5) disbanding? Does a change in mission affect the collaboration's consideration of decision makers, stakeholders, and others? On the other hand, does the collaboration keep abreast of external changes that may introduce new decision makers, stakeholders, or others?

A Checklist

I invite you to put collaboration's life cycle to work by using it as a checklist for identifying strengths, solving problems, and predicting next steps in a collaboration that you are newly joining or one with which you have been long associated.

Copy the following illustration, shown in Figure 6.1, and take it with you to your collaboration's next meeting. Look to see whether the actions inherent and the questions asked in each phase are addressed. Put an "X" through those phases that you think have been addressed well. Put a "?" over those that appear to have been partially or inappropriately addressed. Put an "*" over those that do not appear to have been addressed at all. (Note: This analysis may take more than one meeting!) Once you have completed this exercise, you will have assembled a rough but useful profile of the collaboration and the outline of an agenda for your work as a contributor to the collaboration's success:

- Items marked by "X" are the collaboration's assets. These are the strengths on which to build—and comprise a set of tools that you can use to leverage—additional work in the collaboration.
- Items marked by "?" and "*" are, respectively, the acknowledged opportunities and brand-new tools that can be used over time to strengthen the collaboration.

A Rudimentary Framework

By reflecting on the phases through which most sustained collaborations flow, we create a procedural context for applying the tools of Quality systems alignment. When we connect these phases of collaboration's life cycle to Quality principles, we create—at least in theory—a rudimentary framework for aligning systems through collaboration (see Table 6.1). In theory, this framework can be applied to each goal established by a collaboration. Each cell in this 7×12 matrix challenges us to consider specific actions that need to be planned, executed, and evaluated in order to align systems through collaboration.

The power of this framework emerges when we use its individual cells as tools for planning, managing, and evaluating collaborative systems. Each cell is a bite-size chunk of the larger picture: a finite and targeted element of the complex process of collaborative system alignment. Let's look at three examples (refer also to Table 6.1):

Figure 6.1   Collaboration's Life Cycle

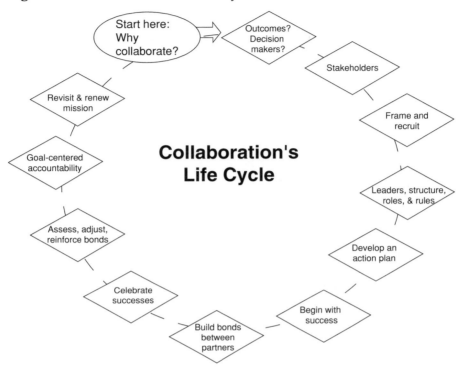

- *Leadership × Why Collaborate.* What is the role of leadership in establishing and communicating the convening vision? What style of leadership is likely to be the most effective? Who should exercise this leadership? Is the collaboration's leadership objective about whether collaboration is essential for accomplishing the convening vision?
- *Fact-Based Decision Making × Develop Action Plan.* What will a meaningful action plan look like? What will be its specific outcomes? What data will we need to develop it? What data will we need to evaluate it? Where will that data come from? How will we collect them? Who will collect them? What will we do with them? What conventions and best practices should we take into consideration?
- *Management Systems × Goal-Centered Accountability.* How will we manage our accountability system? Are there relevant management models for accountability we should employ? Who will manage the accountability system? What resources will be required? How will accountability be integrated into other management systems?

Table 6.1   The Rudiments of a Framework for **Aligning Systems Through Collaboration**

Phases of Collaboration's Life Cycle

Why? [Our shared goals]	What? [Quality principles of system alignment]	Why collaborate?	Outcomes? Decision makers?	Stakeholders?	Frame and recruit	Leaders, structure, roles, & rules	Develop an action plan	Begin with success	Build bonds between partners	Celebrate successes	Assess, adjust, reinforce bonds	Goal-centered accountability	Revisit & renew mission
The outcome(s) we are aiming vto achieve	Leadership	▨											
	Strategic planning												
	Stakeholder focus												
	Fact-based decision making						▨						
	Sensitivity to human resources												
	Management systems											▨	
	Continuous improvement												

I caution the reader that while this is a logical framework, it is untested and warrants further study by researchers, evaluators, and practitioners alike.

* * *

The series of brief essays that follows in Chapter 7 explores the various skills and principles that you and I should understand and employ as we proceed through these phases and set out to become more effective collaborative leaders.

Note

1. Note that these steps are ideally, but not necessarily, a linear sequence (with each step following and depending on the one preceding it). Steps may overlap, repeat, or occur simultaneously. Several steps may not occur until far along the path of a collaboration's life cycle.

7

The Dimensions of Collaborative Leadership

Of Sums and Parts

Collaborative leaders, like the collaborations they help lead, are nearly always greater than the sum of their parts. Because of the synergy of their diverse dimensions, effective collaborative leaders stand out as visionaries, ambitious thinkers, and people with whom others like to associate. Arrogance, insensitivity, aloofness, self-aggrandizement, and the like are barriers to collaboration; people don't want to roll up their sleeves to join in and work alongside others with these characteristics.

The following dimensions are the personal tools that collaborative leaders can use to accomplish collaboration. In a perfect world, all these dimensions combine in the sainted leader whom we follow into the jaws of collaboration. In the real world, they exist to varying degrees. Our very human leaders are certain to be missing several (or many) of these dimensions. These are the ideals toward which we aspire as we strive to improve our abilities to build and lead collaborative initiatives.

It is important to affirm here that collaborative leadership is comprised of skills and characteristics that can be learned. In his book *Leadership Jazz* (1993), Max DePree draws compelling parallels between institutional leaders and jazz musicians who master the basics of their own instruments, practice with their group, and learn the strengths and weaknesses of their musical partners, so that they might improvise together.

As we master our skills as collaborators and jazz musicians, we also learn what to listen for when we hear others play. The remainder of this book is devoted to discussions that introduce the dimensions (or skill sets) that should be present to varying degrees in the partners comprising a collaboration, if the collaboration is to succeed. They are the starting points for self-assessment by collaborative leaders, targets for self-improvement, and skills that we will look (and listen) for in the partners we aim to recruit into our collaborations. At the same time, they constitute an outline of the competencies around which we may begin to build curricula for teaching the skills of collaborative leadership.

For practitioners, these dimensions may well represent our personal, lifelong learning goals. Gathering all these dimensions in one collaboration at one time is the challenge of our professional lifetimes. The best we can do is to first aim for personal mastery of those dimensions that are irreducibly essential and then to work to develop close and sustained leadership relationships with collaborative partners who have and can contribute the missing skills.

For deans and professors in colleges of education, these dimensions contribute to a framework that may guide the development of new curricula and teaching for tomorrow's teachers and school administrators.

For evaluators and researchers, the framework that emerges begs dozens of questions that have not yet been asked and suggests theories that have not yet been explored. There is a research agenda at the core of this work that needs to be tackled with rigor and resources (see Chapter 8).

For teachers, parents, and others who work with children, these dimensions constitute a universe of knowledge and skills that students will need to be effective and collaborative in their lives. Our challenge is to become strategic about building these dimensions into day-to-day life lessons, classroom activities, and formal curricula so that our children become reflective collaborative practitioners.

Twenty-Four Dimensions
of Effective Collaborations

Strategic Thinking

The effective collaborative leader is a strategic, logical, and systemic thinker who understands the steps that must be taken to make things happen and who can engage collaborative partners in a productive and efficient planning process.

For very practical reasons, there is a greater demand for efficiency in collaborative ventures than in individual initiatives. Collaborations cannot be a waste of time. They must produce product, and they must do so in a timely manner; otherwise, partners will quickly see that it makes a great deal more sense to pull back and spend more time on work that must be done in their home organizations.

Planning establishes the basis for both efficiency and accountability; it is the process of translating into action the shared vision that has drawn the several partners together. This is the purpose of planning. All too often, planning is viewed as a cerebral exercise that simply stands in the way of "doing"—there are countless "plans" sitting on bookshelves, gathering dust and bearing witness to the weak consultants and poor planning processes that produced documents disconnected from the practical context of the organization. When done right, planning is the essential and practical process of figuring out how to accomplish a mission.

Planning that is done without direct and routine connection to implementation is not planning at all; it is fiction.

Above all else, strategic thinking and strategic planning are anchored in practicality. They push us to set high goals, then to temper and revise these goals to reflect both our practical capabilities and the learning that takes place as we delve into our issue. For this reason, we generally find (in the words of a good friend) that "deep vision comes in the middle." Through strategic thinking and strategic planning, we acknowledge that we accomplish our mission and goals one student, leader, customer, client, and constituent at a time. Through strategic thinking and planning, we make the connection between the big picture and the individual constituent or customer with the most precision possible . . . ideally, even to the point of naming names. It's not unreasonable for us to expect this of lesson planners in our classrooms; why not also of strategic planners in our collaborative initiatives?

As a strategic thinker, the collaborative leader pays attention to the 12 phases of collaboration's life cycle. Our job is to be alert to our status in that cycle—phases we have passed through, phases in our future—and to be strategic in assessing, planning, and managing this process.

As a strategic thinker, we invest in the strategic attachment of our partners (as does a good teacher). For example,

1. Strategic thinkers make sure that the vision that worked to convene our collaborative partners continues to be viewed as important, timely, and responsive to individual and institutional self-interests by each partner. (We keep our lessons salient, make sure students know why and what they're learning, and—as much as possible—adapt our teaching style to their learning needs.)

2. Strategic thinkers move our partners from vision to action with an action plan comprised of clear-cut achievable steps, outcomes, defined tasks, benchmarks, and accountabilities that are meaningful, along with a process for developing and sustaining momentum. (Many teachers' lesson plans are models of effective action planning for implementing standards and curricular goals.)

3. Strategic thinkers begin with early goals that are meaningful (though modest), achievable, visible, and concretely attached to the self-interests of our partners, then progress to larger, more complex, and transformational goals later when relationships are firmer and the coalition's systems are better established. (This is what is meant by progressive curricula and instruction.)

Asset-Based Perspective

Collaborative leaders are not simply optimists, they are optimizers. They see assets to be aligned where others see disjointed resources and players. They help others see and share a vision of what can be accomplished together where others see a problem to be overcome. They see assets as the foundation on which sustained collaborations are built. An asset-based perspective shapes both the dialog between partners and the targets that they set.[1]

For collaborative leaders, a problem-based or remediation strategy—the opposite of an asset-based perspective—is not always a bad idea. Disasters, disabilities, and deprivation work well to convene and focus people quickly and briefly in collaboration. Think of the heart-wrenching television commercials we've all seen featuring starving children and an announcer's voiceover pleading for contributions. For many people, this problem-based approach works. And it also works for short-term itinerant collaborations aimed at tackling a problem at hand. It is a quick and efficient organizing tool; but it works only on those who are moved by the cause, and only for the duration of their emotional connection.

This short-term problem solving succeeds by triggering an emotion (pity, fear, anger, concern). We can respond by either solving the problem, assuaging the emotion, or finding a way to redirect the emotion (in effect, changing the channel).

An asset-based approach to solving the problem of a teenager's truancy would go beyond the short-term solution of making the teenager show up at school. It would look for reasons to explain the lack of attendance and then work to create a new reality. Collaborative leaders know that real problem solving—real change—involves creating new realities . . . and that this takes time. They work, therefore, toward sustained collaborations that connect partners' self-interests to a shared vision of the reality they can create together . . . for as long as it takes to create it. They convene and hold their collaborative partners together with a proactive vision of what they can do, create, or become.

The other contribution of asset-based thinking to collaborative leadership is its focus on identifying, engaging, integrating, and amplifying the assets that each partner offers to the work of the collaboration. This acknowledges the contribution each partner realistically can make and reinforces the bonds that hold partners in the collaboration.

In addition, an asset-based perspective is coldly analytical, assessing what assets will be needed to get the job done, what assets are represented within the collaboration's membership, what assets exist hidden within the community that have never before been tapped, and what assets are missing that must then be recruited or otherwise gathered to accomplish the goal(s) of the collaboration.

Professional Credibility

It is important that collaborative leaders be viewed as credible colleagues. Credibility is earned by having (1) substantive mastery, (2) peer status, and (3) professional integrity.

The purpose of professional Credibility is to validate the appropriateness and generate confidence in your professional colleagues' decisions to join a portion of their visions and reputations with you, to get professional colleagues to invest first in you and then with you at the level you need to accomplish a desired purpose.

In a practical sense, you do not need to be more expert or smarter than your prospective collaborative partners; they simply need to view you as credible.

The components of Credibility are:

1. *Substantive mastery.* This consists of the baseline knowledge that professionals expect of effective colleagues in their field. Stated otherwise, a professional whose substantive competence is either questionable or an embarrassment to colleagues will fight an uphill battle to gather colleagues willingly around a vision.

2. *Peer status.* It is generally, and tediously, true that peers must convene peers and therefore collaborative leaders must be of at least the same status within our home organizations as those we would convene. Moreover, once the collaboration has been initiated and institutional representatives have begun meeting, it is important that collaborative leaders pay close attention to the possibility of *status erosion*. Status erosion begins when one institutional partner delegates representation to a person within his or her organization of lower status than the original representative without consensual agreement of all partners. In some professions and climates, this may produce a domino effect in which the remaining institutional partners react by reassigning and reducing the status of their representatives to the collaboration.

3. *Professional integrity.* This applies the concept of integrity specifically to the professional context and has a separate meaning of integrity, than that described later (in the discussion of Integrity). It is measured by codes of ethics, professional standards, and compliance with the principles and normative values associated with being, for example, an educator or administrator.

It is important to remember that for collaborative leaders, Credibility, like beauty, is in the eyes of a fickle and constantly reappraising beholder. If our professional stature is brought into question or if the work of the collaboration falters in a fashion attributable to our leadership; if deadlines aren't met or promises aren't kept and we can be faulted; if a collaborative partner feels that the progress of the collaboration does not justify his or her continued involvement; then, naturally, our Credibility as a collaborative leader is threatened. Beyond ensuring that we strive to achieve the TQM adage of surpassing customer expectations, there are at least three routes to protecting and bolstering what we may call *Process Credibility*:

1. Invest in your professional stature. Make sure you do nothing that could be construed as professionally questionable or embarrassing by your colleagues. And stay on top of your field through professional development, education, and research.

2. Develop ground rules, expectations, and benchmarks early on that establish mutual accountabilities for the administrative and substantive progress of the collaboration. The ground rules and expectations should be adopted by consensus, not by a majority (majority approval means that the fundamental operations of the collaboration have been rejected by a minority of participants). These ground rules broaden and specify the mutual responsibilities of all partners. In the absence of such assignments, all the work of the collaboration naturally filters back to the collaborative leader. Even with these protections, collaborative leaders are responsible for following up and ensuring that partners comply with the ground rules, accept assignments, and meet deadlines.

3. Recruit at least one or two highly visible civic or institutional leaders with high Credibility, high status, and in whom you have high confidence that their commitment to the collaboration will result in their sustained and steady involvement. The involvement of partners of this type will go a long way to enhance your Credibility and to lengthen the patience of other partners.

Timing the Launch

Whether a collaboration is launched in response to a crisis or to plan and carry out a long-standing vision, the timing of its launch will influence who comes on board and how best to organize the initiative.

It goes without saying that the process of building a collaborative initiative never happens in a void. Social, political, professional, personal, and (sometimes) even meteorological conditions affect the readiness of prospective partners to join and work together. (Try launching a new arts and culture collaboration while the National Guard is airlifting people from the roofs of their flooded homes!)

The collaborative leader controls the launch of the collaboration. By this I mean that the leader controls the time and conditions under which partners are convened to begin the process of building the collaborative initiative. The launching phase is a sensitive and important time because the purpose of the collaboration has not yet been clearly defined, institutional relationships are still generally undefined, and few if any individuals or organizations have made a commitment to the collaboration as a vehicle for addressing the convening issue (except, perhaps, you as the collaborative leader). At this phase, the rationality of Reinhold Niebuhr's Serenity Prayer may guide our collaborative leadership:

> God, give us grace to accept with serenity the things that cannot be changed, courage to change the things which should be changed, and the wisdom to distinguish the one from the other.

To time the launch of a collaborative initiative, we need to understand and gauge the implications of the variety of environmental conditions that may affect the outcomes of our efforts. Those conditions that we cannot change we must accept and work around. But those conditions that we can change (by our direct impact; our ability to influence others' perceptions of those conditions; or our patient waiting for conditions to shift, evolve, pass, or otherwise change through natural means) demand our strategic attention.

As collaborative leaders, we've timed the launch not only on the basis of these environmental concerns but also on the basis of having taken the time to envision the goal we are aiming to achieve and then working backwards through the sequence of steps that will likely be needed to accomplish it. This gives us the advantage of being able to realistically estimate (1) what the collaboration will need to accomplish first, second, and third and (2) when we will need to convene in order to meet realistic time frames for accomplishing each successive stage.

Recruiting the Right Mix

Nothing shapes the culture, process, and outcomes of a collaborative initiative as much as decisions related to who is asked to join it.

One of the biggest challenges facing collaborative leaders is successfully identifying and recruiting the right collaborative partners.

The rational universe of prospective partners in our collaborations draws from the two sources of decision makers and stakeholders described in the discussion of collaboration's life cycle in Chapter 6.

The dimensions discussed in this chapter outline considerations for identifying and recruiting decision makers and stakeholders on the basis of substantive and individual contributions each may make to achieving the collaboration's goals. Remember, in the best of circumstances we are looking to find each of these 24 dimensions resident in our collaborations and/or in the skill sets of our collaborations' partners.

Our ability to identify controlling decision makers is determined first and foremost by how clear we are about what we are aiming to achieve. Once we are clear on intended outcomes, we can readily identify controlling interests. We have, then, some basic research questions:

- Where (in what institution) does the authority reside to take a needed action, make a critical decision, or allocate an essential resource?
- Who within that institution has the authority to make that decision?
- What individuals and conditions affect this decision maker? (This raises the issue of webs of influence.)

The answers to these questions will produce a pool of controlling decision makers and individuals who have the capacity to influence these decision makers. Once we've prioritized this pool and set our sights on prospective partners, the challenge is to work through all "seven degrees of separation" to ascertain how close we can come to communicating directly (or indirectly) with our targeted prospects, and then develop strategies for reaching them.

To identify the pool of stakeholders in our collaborative purpose, our question is: What other individuals and institutions have a history and stake in the issue or outcomes we are pursuing? This is both an historical and a survey question:

- What other organizations and individuals would benefit directly or indirectly from the work of the collaboration?
- Are there organizations and individuals whose knowledge of either the issues or the decision makers command their participation in the collaborative venture?

- Are there organizations and individuals whose reputation and prestige would either improve the collaboration's capacity to influence decision makers, other stakeholders, or constituencies—or who would be especially notable in their absence?
- Are there organizations and individuals with sufficient history related to the collaborative purpose that their absence from the collaboration would signal (or suggest) a purposeful break with them?
- Are there organizations or individuals whose participation must be considered if for no other reason than the ability or power they may have to thwart the work of the collaboration?
- Are there organizations and individuals who could work compatibly and productively within the collaboration and whose involvement would somehow reduce or obviate certain known or predictable opposition to the collaboration?
- Are there organizations and individuals who have resources that are needed by the collaboration (resources that are not available elsewhere) but that, otherwise, have no stakeholding interest in the collaboration? Collaborative leaders are especially challenged to recruit these targets either by paying for their services (essentially making them financial stakeholders) or by entrepreneurially crafting a new connection of their mission-driven self-interests and the goal(s) of the collaboration.

Some central principles are at the core of starting out right. We should begin by building the core of our collaborations with individuals and institutional representatives

- Whom we trust and with whom work well; in other words, relationships we have already built
- For whom the agenda/problem/need to be tackled clearly and unquestionably overlaps with their missions and self-interests
- Who are the least controversial (or at least represent the least unnecessary controversy) within the universe of constituencies associated with the agenda/problem/need
- Who are of high enough profile and Credibility to attract and reinforce the involvement of other targeted partners

These conditions will allow us to build the initial core of our collaboration with partners who have an affinity for our issue and leadership, are inherently attuned and committed to the issue, and are not likely to limit our ability to attract other partners or predispose the membership and capacity of the collaboration to one particular constituency or perspective.

Remember that we are recruiting collaborative partners to strengthen us, not replicate us. We are recruiting them to build a broadly harmonic collection of voices singing the same tune. This metaphor is an important reminder for all collaborative leaders during our recruitment phase. The significance of "harmony" emerges from its very definition. Diversity is inherent and essential for harmony. Without differences in the timbre and tone of the various participants, we end up with monotonic sound, little more than a somewhat louder version of a single voice singing.

Interpersonal Communication Skills

Communication sits at the center of all human relationships. Collaboration, as relationship management, demands the skillful use of interpersonal communication.

Our job, as collaborative leaders, is to work to develop a climate in which honest and productive communication occurs among partners. We contribute to this

- By modeling honest and productive communication skills
- By asking more questions than we answer
- By attentively working to ensure all partners participate in key discussions
- By noting and addressing nonparticipation
- By never permitting decisions to be made by tacit endorsement but, rather, by making sure that each partner is engaged in the decision with (at least) an active vote or affirmation of support

Within the collaboration, all communication must be purposeful, reciprocal, accessible, honest, and succinct.[2]

Consensus Building

Consensus Building connects the individual and institutional self-interests of partners to the goals and activities of the collaboration.

This dimension is closely associated with the group-facilitator function of Group Process and draws heavily from the Psychosocial and Entrepreneurial dimensions (see sections that follow).

Some collaborations work well within a consensus model; some succeed by following a majoritarian model. Whether a collaboration takes action only if every participant agrees to the action or acts when a majority of participants vote to take action, it is always beneficial in public sector collaborations for leaders to have the skills to build the largest possible consensus around action before it is taken.

The foundation for building consensus is laid when we have articulated one or more goals that clearly, meaningfully, and simply connect the self-interests of our partners to the purpose of the collaboration. There can be no ambiguity (no flexibility that allows for undue reinterpretation down the road); the connection must be significant enough to warrant the commitment; and the statement of goals should be memorable and compelling, like a well-honed slogan. Meaningful truths are elegantly concise and simple, which is good, since simply stated truths make better organizing tools—symbols around which we can build consensus and return to, routinely, to validate the consensus we have built. Remember our discussion of Alinsky's lesson that the simple stop sign makes a better organizing tool than would the complex challenge of eradicating a neighborhood's rats.

Lyndon Johnson's approach to building consensus is said to have involved gathering his advisors together in a locked conference room, posing the question for which he needed an answer, filling and refilling their coffee cups often, and then not unlocking the door to the bathrooms until consensus was reached. There are, of course, less torturous strategies we can use. But whatever the strategy, five principles should guide our leadership as consensus builders:

- If you can't be clear on the intended outcome, be clear on the question you want answered. Our job, as collaborative leaders, is to move our group step-by-step toward our goals. Given the expertise that resides within the membership of our collaborations, our best role may be to pose questions that evoke the distillation of complex issues into bite-size achievable decisions around which we can facilitate consensus-building discussion.
- See the world through the eyes of those you would influence. We cannot find a way to connect our partners' self-interests to a decision until we understand how they perceive and react to the question.
- Tenacity. There is an adage that the Great Wall of China can be brought down with a ping-pong ball, if one tosses it against

the wall time and again until a weakness is found. Our job as collaborative leaders beckons us to be persistent, push for consensus, and persist in shaping and adapting the question and the environment until (finally) a satisfying decision that responds to our colleagues' self-interests can be reached.

- Be an advocate for the collaboration, not for any one decision. As collaborative leaders, we are the ones who are most invested in the health and success of the collaboration. And, while passions may run high on any one question or decision facing our group, we should be the ones to whom our colleagues can turn for leadership and advocacy on behalf of the whole collaboration. Collaborative leaders have a duty to be cautious of when and how we advocate specific policy positions or courses of action within our collaborations.

- When you hit a snag, isolate the objection. There will be times when conflicting self-interests among collaborative partners will make consensus seem all but impossible. When this happens, we should take a lesson from sales and negotiation strategies: Ask for and isolate the objection. Narrow the focus of the conflict until it is clearly identified and isolated. Then present the objection clearly to ensure its validity for both parties. At this point you may determine that language (the words used to define a position) may be the sticking point. If this is the case, then experiment with language until you can generate agreement on terms. If the objection is more substantial, then establish its linkages to other elements in the transaction. Is the element in question so important to the final outcome that it must be included, or can it simply be dropped and, thereby, resolved at no cost? Can it be traded for a party's self-interest that is of lower priority for the success of the collaboration? If so, make the tradeoff clear to at least the two parties involved so that the conflict does not crop up again in another context.

Diplomacy

Collaborative leaders face the diplomatic challenge of striking a sustainable balance between the interests of individual member institutions and the interests of the collaboration as a whole.

Of the many bumps in the road that the collaborative leader must negotiate, the most universal and contentious can be the relationship of the identity of the whole versus the identity of the individual member. It is safe to say that few institutional leaders will sacrifice the good of their home organizations for the benefit of an external collaboration. The diplomatic function of a collaborative leader is to strike an ongoing balance between competing and evolving interests. This includes making sure that

1. The collaboration never goes into head-to-head competition with an institutional partner for funding, public profile, or any other significant and potentially threatening element of an institution's identity and survival.

2. The mission of the collaboration never overlaps so dramatically with that of any one institutional partner as to raise legitimate doubt of the need for both entities.

3. The activities of the collaboration never surprise decision makers or stakeholders associated with any of the partners or the larger constituency of the collaboration. Timely communication and attention to cultivating mutual confidence are central elements of diplomacy.

As a rule, a collaboration's activities should be seen by all participants as the coordination of projects and activities that each partner would have dreamed of doing independently . . . although with less effect.

Every effort should be made to illustrate the degree to which collaborative initiatives integrate and reinforce the efforts of our collaborative partners and to mitigate against a collaboration's activities ever being viewed by its partners as competing for time or financial resources with their own institutions' activities. (See the related discussion about the environmental engineer function of the Group Process domain.)

This principle applies equally to emerging and pre-existing collaborations. Whether the function of the collaboration is to stimulate and provide a forum for planning new initiatives that go beyond the capacity of individual members or to extend the mission or programs of institutional partners in some progressive fashion, care should be taken to adopt new projects only after they have been (1) circulated among all collaborative partners and relevant decision makers in their organizations and (2) authorized by each collaborating partner as an approved project or program in keeping with their professional self-interests and institutional mission. (Other steps that may help ensure broad ownership and comfort with the collaboration's new initiatives include (3) asking partners to show and discuss how the collaboration's initiative fits into and contributes to their own operating plans and (4) establishing a budgeting procedure that has each partner formally contribute human or material resources, or both, to the success of the joint initiative.)

A final, inherent quality of our concept of diplomacy is the vision-driven selflessness of leadership. By this I mean simply to acknowledge that effective collaborative leaders spread the credit among all the collaborative partners for any successes or good decisions of the collaboration. As collaborative leaders, our egos should be attached to the successes of the campaign, not to taking credit for them. Throughout the process of building and managing relationships, nothing binds people to a relationship or a process quite so well as evidence that their comments, suggestions, and brilliant recommendations are taken seriously in the relationship and, one way or another, are highlighted or actualized in the process of the campaign. At the same time, few things will chip away at the ego gratification offered by a relationship more than the gnawing feeling that one party to it is simply a cipher, rubber stamp, or window dressing in a process dominated and manipulated by the ideas of one other person. No matter how brilliant we are or how dull and uncreative our partners may be, if we have chosen our partners for valid reasons, then our responsibility as the relationship manager is to create an environment in which each partner has good reason to believe that his or her ideas are desired, valued, valuable, and acted on.[3]

Understanding the Rudiments of Each Sector

Effective collaborative leaders not only reach beyond the limits of their own organizations but also reach across professions and the boundaries that define the nonprofit, government, and for-profit sectors. Most of us need to expand our limited knowledge of others' professions and the other sectors to be able to find mutual self-interests, build effective relationships, and understand the conditions that affect the decisions and needs of our collaborative partners.

To be effective collaborative leaders, we don't need to be expert in the legal, social, historical, and cultural elements of the professions, organizations, and sectors from which our collaborative colleagues come. But we do need working insights to be knowledgeable of the institutional contexts that shape our partners' interests and perspectives as they work in the collaboration, for two reasons, as indicated on the next page.

1. In a manner of speaking, we need to be able to look through the eyes of our colleagues to see ourselves and our collaboration as each collaborative partner sees us and our collaboration.

2. We need to be sensitive regarding the culture, ethos, and needs of the professions and organizations that our colleagues represent so that we may engage and respond to them with understanding and respect.

Seeing the world through our colleagues' eyes (point 1 above) is a parallel skill to understanding our partners' self-interests. Both are essential if we are to successfully engage them in our collaboration and make their participation productive. Institutional representatives see us as a vehicle for accomplishing something for their institutions. We need to know what that something is. Moreover, institutional representatives carry into the collaboration not only specific goals from their home institutions but also policies, politics, reporting relationships, time frames for getting things done, and other influences from their home institutions that shape what they expect from the collaboration, how they view it, and how they operate within it. Here's a simple illustration of what some of these differences might be:

> Partners who come from entrepreneurial for-profit businesses, where decisions are made quickly on the basis of clear-cut bottom-line criteria, may be most comfortable in a collaborative environment that is fast-paced, formal, quantitative . . . and that meets at 6:00 a.m., before the workday begins. Partners coming from education and nonprofit institutions, where decisions are often participatory and mission driven, may attach themselves with more conviction to collaborations that tap and stroke their affective connection to people, goals, vision . . . and that begin at 5:30 p.m., just before their round of late-night community meetings. Partners who are volunteers—with day jobs and families—are going to come with widely varied perspectives and decision-making needs . . . and may best be able to attend meetings that begin at 7:30 p.m., after dinner and homework and just slightly before exhaustion sets in.

The respect that is born of knowledge about others and their contexts (point 2 above) is a vital element of this dimension. We respect people who respect us. And no right-minded person would willingly volunteer to follow a collaborative leader whose behavior or lack of knowledge suggested disrespect. But in the stereotypic shorthand to which we all fall victim, educators and nonprofit people have little respect for the self-serving ruthlessness of business people, business people have little respect for the mushy soft-headedness of soft-hearted educators and nonprofit people, and no one has respect for the heart-lessness and blundering inefficiency of government bureaucrats. As someone who has been all three, I promise any doubters that these stereotypes are no more true of the other sectors than they are of yours.

It should go without saying that effective collaborative leaders can never permit themselves to fall victim to this kind of sloppy worldview. But, almost every year, the fundamental disrespect of some significant leader is exposed by a hidden microphone or video camera that captures a slur, an epithet, or a demeaning joke. We ridicule leaders who inappropriately stereotype and demean people because of what they do for a living just as we attack leaders who expose themselves as racist, sexist, or otherwise bigoted. This is the way it should be.

Data-Driven Leadership

In the 21st century, data rules. Technology is an unrelenting task-master that drives leaders and educators to numbers, research, and best practices. Intuition is a resource for decision makers, but never again will it be sufficient justification for leading organizational change.

Edward Deming played a big role in leading modern manage-ment to decision-making models that are research based, data driven, and devoted to best practice. Contemporary Quality principles are predicated on this. In collaborations, this is particularly important.

For whatever reasons our collaborations exist, they must satisfy their connections to partners' self interests by being successful and efficient in what they do. If they don't succeed in a timely fashion, then partners will seek other means toward their desired ends. If they cost too much—in terms of time, money, human resources, political capital, and the like—then partners will abandon them as well. Research, data, and best practices are the tools that enable collabora-tions to decide to act in ways that increase both the likelihood of suc-cess and the efficiency of the effort.

Collaborative leaders view knowledge of research, data, and best practices as a resource that must be present among or accessible to the members of their collaborations. We look for this knowledge—and cultivate it—in our stakeholders, or we otherwise recruit or purchase it so it becomes part of how we operate. Collaborative leaders make commitment to data-driven leadership part of the conversation, plan-ning, and work of their collaborations.

Psychosocial: Understanding People

While collaborations generally link institutions, the institutional decision to join is made by individuals. And, as each institutional partner chooses the person who will represent it in the collaboration, the commitment and style of that selected representative will largely define the quality and influence of each institution's participation.

The most elemental skill required of collaborative leaders is the interpersonal skill and empathy needed to make and sustain strong linkages between people. This tool begins with a built-in radar that detects the personal self-interests people bring into a relationship, deduces each person's level of commitment to the relationship, and observes and interprets the relevant psychosocial rhythms and styles of each individual. Effective leaders, in any context, understand the character, needs, work styles, capacities, and self-interests of the people with whom they work.

This leadership challenge is more complicated for collaborative leaders because we are not only dealing with individuals as complex psychosocial organisms but also as representatives of complex institutions with highly individualized structures, needs, histories, and institutional self-interests.

Collaborative partners connect with the collaboration at two levels:

> The first is at the level of mission. In the individual, this is the "must have" attachment, an affiliation that one is compelled to have because it is either (1) so obviously attached to the spiritual or professional identity of the individual that it is inconceivable (or would be terribly embarrassing) that this person would not affiliate or (2) in the institutional interest of an organization that delegates its affiliation to an individual representative. This is what brings individuals to the collaboration table in the first place.
>
> The second is at the level of individual needs. This is the dimension that grows from the collaborative leader's effectiveness at getting the individual feeling good and well rewarded by his or her involvement in the collaboration. This is what determines the level of energy and engagement each individual exercises in the collaboration.

As collaborative leaders, we are always aware that people representing institutions within a collaboration are regularly balancing what they would like to do—taking positions and making decisions that would satisfy their own personal self-interests—with what they know they should do in their representational capacity—taking positions and making decisions that serve their institutions' best interests. This is a constant internal negotiation in which an institutional representative may be just as likely to sacrifice a particular self-interest to meet an institutional need as to take action that would serve a self-interest if it can be rationalized by mildly stretching and interpreting his or her institution's interests. Effective collaborative leaders know that collaborative partners often interpret (if not shape) their institutions' interests in the collaboration.

Institutionalizing the Worry

This is perhaps the most undervalued, often ignored, and important dimension of collaborative leadership.

It is the dimension that guarantees that somebody is worried about the success of the collaboration (that the collaboration will not disintegrate for lack of attention). It is a self-possessed tenacity on the part of the collaborative leader to make sure that the collaborative venture is fed, nourished, and attended to during each phase of its development. It is figuratively—if not formally—written into the job description of the collaborative leader or a delegated agent.

It is the practical response to the acknowledged truth that if no one person accepts responsibility for the success of any process, cause, project, or collaborative initiative, then surely it will be displaced to lower and lower levels on everyone's list of priorities until, at last, it disappears altogether. This is especially true in collaborations since all institutional representatives have primary responsibility and loyalty to their home institutions.

Because each partner's priority is with his or her home institution—accomplishing its institutional mission, attending to its day-to-day managerial responsibilities, and ensuring its financial solvency and growth—only the partner whose institutional mission overlaps most extensively with the mission of the collaboration will have the luxury of deciding to expend extensive amounts of personal and institutional resources to support the work of the collaboration. Collaborations that are "staffed" by such a partner agency are challenged to reduce the appearance and fact that the collaboration exists simply as an opportunistic extension of that one partner's own program operations. Short-term collaborations, organized around immediate and critical issues, can usually succeed as extensions of one credible institutional partner. The challenge arises for sustained collaborations in which the ongoing primacy and influence of one partner reduces the co-equal sense of investment, ownership, and responsibility among the other partners.

At the opposite extreme, collaborative efforts that are highly democratic and totally voluntaristic run into their own, often fatal, problem: When no one person is responsible for managing and building the collaboration, the collaboration fails under the weight of its universally second-priority status. Calling meetings, preparing materials, making phone calls, writing proposals, meeting deadlines, and all the other sustaining administrative elements of a collaboration don't get done unless it is in somebody's "job description" to get them done. The best-laid plans and the most fervent commitments made by the most well-intentioned collaborative partners will nearly always be secondary to the crisis, deadline, meeting, and "stuff" that occurs within their own families and organizations for which they are accountable.

One person—with Credibility in the eyes of each of the collaborative partners, stature sufficient to deal directly with appropriate personnel in each of the collaborative institutions, proven capacity to administer the collaboration, and a passionate commitment to the mission of the collaboration—needs to worry about (and be responsible for) managing and growing the collaboration. The success of any sustained collaboration rests, in large part, on "institutionalizing the worry" in a single competent administrative coordinator. Collaborations vary as to whether this coordinator assumes the public role of spokesperson or behind-the-scenes administrator. In either case, it is this person's competence in planning, managing, and developing the collaboration that defines the collaboration's capacity to make significant progress toward its mission.

Until you hire paid staff, the work of the collaboration will always be everybody's second (or third!) priority—except, perhaps, yours. Every partner is, first, an officer in an institution, a teacher in a classroom, and/or a parent of children. As central as the mission of the collaboration may become in their lives, we can never count on another to care as much for the success of the collaboration as we do. The buck stops with us (even as the glory will go to all the collaborative partners). So roll up your sleeves and pay attention . . . more attention than anybody else.

Group Process

The effective collaborative leader is (1) an environmental engineer, (2) a group facilitator, and, all too often, (3) a grunt operative.

If we don't pay attention to the functional dynamics of the group—either by attending to them ourselves or by being responsible for ensuring that other colleagues in the collaboration pick up pieces of this responsibility—then the collaboration will fail. All three responsibilities—as environmental engineer, group facilitator, and grunt operative—are nearly always required, although our role as environmental engineer becomes both more important and complex the longer the intended duration of our collaboration.

Our role as environmental engineer entails both a body of skills and character traits that enable collaborative leaders to create an environment in which people learn enough about each other to care about each other and to want to help each other—and each other's institutions—succeed. This can be as important a glue as are vision and goals in getting the individuals who represent the institutional partners to want to work together and to be sufficiently invested in the success of the collaboration to make the effort to overcome its many challenges.

This is the element of collaborative leadership that cynics and "Lone Rangers" deplore. Building and sustaining a network of collaborative partners naturally takes more work and, perhaps, more time than tackling the same issue on your own. It also increases the number of stakeholders (those invested in its success) and escalates its profile, impact, resources, and pool of prospective beneficiaries. It demands a conscientious effort to build a climate of mutual trust and comfort, a culture that fosters honest engagement, open communication, and diplomatically couched hardball regarding what will work, what won't, who really ought to talk to whom, when, how, and so forth. It calls, also, for finding ways to recognize and reinforce individuals' behaviors and initiatives that benefit the collaboration. Celebrating successes and rewarding contributions are important parts of this process. In bygone days, the predominantly male leadership circles of large associations and corporations resisted this type of social engineering, viewing it as soft and unessential, as embracing the maternal characteristics of nesting, nurturing, and launching.

In collaborations, we move beyond this by celebrating the success of the collaboration and acknowledging the successes of individual partners. This distinction is important for collaborative leaders who, unlike institutional leaders, are in the constant business of building and reinforcing something that exists only by virtue of the collective vision and voluntarism of its participants (unlike institutions with their legalities, structured management and decision-making systems, histories, etc.). Institutional leaders have the luxury of being able to reward and reinforce each individual's performance to breed an environment in which individuals strive. We have the responsibility of building an environment in which the power of collective action is recognized, reinforced, and elevated as a driving motive and key to success.

If we succeed in building this environment, then interpersonal, interinstitutional, and intrainstitional politics are pretty much left at the door as we strive to make sure that meetings of the collaboration benefit from honest and informed discussion, insights, and action with no fear that underlying political agendas are really at play. Underlying this dimension is our ability to create an environment of dignity and respect. As environmental engineers, an important tool is our own behavior and role modeling (that is, for example, whatever we may think of the individual character, skills, competence, or even a specific idea of a particular partner, we're obliged to make sure that our body language and other communications convey clear and consistent respect for the individual).

Our role as group facilitator entails planning and running meetings, communicating between meetings to make sure that assignments are carried out, keeping the energy and spirit of the group positive and fulfilling, keeping politics that may exist (interpersonal and interinstitutional) to a minimum and controlled within our meetings, and so forth. The role of group facilitator is critically important in collaborations since most collaborations do their planning, goal setting, and action steps during meetings of the collaborative partners (whereas most organizations assign elements of these critical decisions to staff or to committees). Each of us, whether serving as chair of the meeting or as one of several collaborative partners around the table, has a stake in—and a responsibility for—ensuring effective, productive, and well-facilitated meetings.

Some startup collaborations choose to contract-out for meeting facilitators (or recruit outside volunteers) in order to ensure (1) high productivity, (2) evenhandedness in managing give-and-take during discussions, or (3) that no one participant has undue influence over the course of discussion. Others establish self-conscious routines for rotating the meeting-management role so that all participants play it equally. The truth be known, peer pressure and the bright light of running a meeting that both involves all our partners and is being observed by all our partners virtually reduces to zero the undue influence any one of us can effectively have as the group facilitator. The real hidden influence is the one known to attorneys since the first contract was carved in stone: The person who controls the final write-up of whatever was discussed and agreed on during a meeting (the summary, proposal, or draft of language that will be used) can profoundly influence the interpretation, skew, and direction of the next steps that will be taken.

Meeting-management skills are at the core of the group facilitator role. It's a simple truth that, if the meetings we call are not efficient and productive, we will quickly lose key partners to their other (more productive) responsibilities. Not surprisingly, these skills are more complicated for us than they are for institutional leaders because we do not enjoy the status differential within a collaboration that gives institutional leaders added and immediate authority within their own meetings. In other words, meeting management among people of equal status is different than meeting management involving people from different levels of vertical hierarchies. Teachers and principals, for example, are used to the added clout that status gives them in the group activities that they routinely manage. As we shift from our workplace into our leadership roles in our collaborations, we must consciously make concomitant shifts in our mindsets and communications. For example, saying "please play nicely" can almost always be seen as a friendly plea (perhaps from an equal), while "don't fight" will almost always be received as an admonition or threat from someone with greater power.

What follows are some generic ground rules for preparing ourselves to lead meetings (of two or more people) toward our intended collaborative outcomes.

Ground Rules for Effective Meeting Management

1. Be very clear just why you are meeting. What is your targeted outcome? What is it you want to accomplish?

2. Be alert to all levels of feedback from all corners of the room. Like actors on a stage, each item of feedback—each stimulus —becomes your cue for a response that is intended to stimulate a desired reaction on the part of your partner(s). You are leading others consciously toward a conclusion (the targeted outcome) and unconsciously toward feeling good about partnering with you. Relationship management is an iterative process: You are the partner whose job it is to consciously reflect on the stimuli you receive and to strategically control the stimuli you introduce by your reactions.

3. Master and take ownership of your own management skills. Don't permit your excellent interpersonal skills to fall victim

to ineffectual organizational skills. Learn (for instance) how to run tightly structured outcome-oriented meetings. Understand and build experience in strategic planning, project management, budgeting, and the like. Find the organizational management skills in which you are good and build your confidence in them—build relationships with colleagues who excel in your weaknesses so you can become more confident in these areas.

4. Ensure your personal mastery of the material at hand. Even if your contribution to the collaborative partnership is not substantive expertise (if you are, for instance, a policymaker whose contribution is clout in a collaboration built to shape legislation), don't expect the meeting to be a personal tutorial session. Do your homework! Learn enough to reasonably level the substantive playing field and to ensure a reasonable comfort level in your dealings with colleagues. Nothing will reduce your ability to pay attention to all the interpersonal nuances of relationship management more than having to struggle to overcome the tension created by your personal inadequacy in holding up your end of substantive discussion during the meeting. Understand all you can about the subject and your collaborative partners so you can interpret, cultivate, and influence the best contribution each partner can make.

5. Prepare twice for each meeting. Always go into meetings with an alternative or backup agenda in mind. This is especially important in the early phases of building a relationship or a collaborative initiative involving multiple relationships because you do not yet have enough data to consistently predict the behavior of the other party or parties and therefore don't know what challenges might be placed before the primary agenda you hope to accomplish. Always have a bottom line, a minimum outcome, to fall back on (that is, a satisfying outcome that may be less than desired but still indicative of progress).

* * *

Note that the group facilitator function exposes not only our meeting-management skills but also our human relations skills for all the world (or, at least, our collaborative partners) to see. How well we can predict, guide, and manage the behaviors of others will predict our ability to facilitate productive meetings. And, as is true in most

Box 7.1

Beware:

The Malicious Saboteur: A prospective partner whose institutional affiliation is appropriate but who harbors—and acts upon—personal animus toward some central figure in the collaboration.

The Limelight Saboteur: Someone who can't function as a co-equal within the partnership but who must be the one whose name, face, and title are at the center of the collaboration's public image and internal discussion.

The Power-Grabbing Saboteur: Although sharing some common themes with the Limelight Saboteur, this prospective partner will not participate unless he or she controls the power to make decisions. This may stem from either arrogance, a personal need for power, a directive from his or her home institution establishing such power control as a prerequisite for participation, or distrust of the leadership provided by the convening collaborative leader.

The Lone Wolf Saboteur: This person joined the collaboration with no institutional affiliation—perhaps because of his or her expertise, history of attachment to the convening issue, public visibility, or friendship with an influential partner—and weighs in on issues, discussions, and decisions with the same power, vote, and influence as institutional representatives but without the same accountability, connection with practicality, or ability to contribute resources to the work of the collaboration.

The Ambivalent Saboteur: This institutional partner is not fully committed to the mission or process of the collaboration, participates sporadically, and may send different representatives to the collaboration's meetings.

The Sloppy-Thinking or Distracted Saboteur: This partner doesn't pay enough attention, reacts only to the immediate point under discussion (often with great passion that diverts discussion in unproductive directions), is seemingly always disconnected or distracted, doesn't know what's going on, is argumentative

or makes recommendations devoid of context and with little
bearing on the subject at hand, and often persists on redundantly
returning discussion to the rudiments or controversies dealt
with at the very beginning of the collaboration's life.

As a general rule of thumb, if we have (1) built among our collaborative partners an earnest belief that they have a stake in the
success of the collaboration (that is, succeeded in connecting the
work of the collaboration to their personal and institutional self-
interests) and (2) created an environment within our collaboration
that both enables and expects direct and honest communication
between partners, then other leaders among our collaborative
partners will be motivated to help us confront and manage the
saboteurs.

any context, our skills as group facilitator will nearly always be most
tested in the breach—when saboteurs arise to do mischief and to challenge the productivity (and survival) of our collaborations. Box 7.1
contains a partial list of what to look out for.

Our role as grunt operative includes everything from mailing
agendas and notices of meetings to doing research, creating discussion drafts, copying material, and arranging for refreshments. These
functions may be assumed by a volunteer or staff person assigned to
the collaboration or as a contribution to the collaboration by one or
more of its institutional members. But because collaborations are
generally lean operations and are often ad hoc, these maintenance
and clerical functions that are taken for granted in our offices must
be strategically attended to in our collaborations—and that attention
won't be paid by anyone unless the collaborative leader—assuming
the function of the *Institutional Worry*—ensures that it is paid.

Resource Development

This is a straightforward dimension of any contemporary leadership
post, but it is more complicated when applied to collaborations
because of our responsibility to enhance the capacity of our collaborative partners and to never hurt or impede their ability to raise the
resources they need for their home institutions.

As collaborative leaders, we have to know how to find the
resources we will need to get the job done from traditional and

nontraditional sources, from inside and outside the collaboration. Certainly, this entails skills of researching, cultivating, soliciting, negotiating, reporting, and sustaining monetary and in-kind contributions. The added complexity is hinted at in the earlier discussion of Diplomacy: In the competitive marketplace of corporate, government, and foundation philanthropy, not only is it self-destructive for collaborations to ever compete with any of their members for funding, but collaborations also have the inherent responsibility to enhance the capacity of member institutions to meet their institutional goals.

Successful collaborative leaders build a sense of shared responsibility among all the partners for generating the resources needed to ensure the success of the collaboration. When we are successful in creating environments characterized by trust and commitment to the success of the collaboration (see the discussion of the environmental engineer under the Group Process dimension), then it follows that our partners will accept this shared responsibility and will participate in, and contribute to, resource-generating activities on behalf of the collaboration. Once we have achieved this environment of trust, as well as the confidence of each partner that the collaboration serves their appropriate self-interests, then our partners may well tolerate some risk by permitting the collaboration to enter the fray for competitive grants from traditional philanthropies.

Other options available to some collaborations include dues structures, fees for membership services, charging "commission" on money saved through collaborative programs (such as joint purchasing), drawing overhead from grants, and other revenue generated by programs undertaken by the collaboration.

Marketing/Communications

Marketing is the planned and managed dialog between a corporate entity's internal and external decision makers, stakeholders, and customers. "Communications" is the name we give to the same function in the public sector. Our job as collaborative leaders is to make sure that this dialog is productive, timely, and inclusive.

As we build our collaboration, this dialog fulfills important internal and external purposes.

Internal Purposes

A routine and accurate record of actions and decisions of the collaboration is an important tool for making sure that all decision makers and stakeholders within partnering organizations share a fact-based understanding of the work of the collaboration. The benefits of this are at least threefold:

1. Open, accurate communications (baring warts and all) minimize both the perception and the opportunity for behind-the-scenes politics within the collaboration.

2. Providing such a running record to each collaborative partner encourages regular and aggressive communications back into partnering organizations . . . nearly always an asset for ensuring strong linkages between partners and the collaboration.

3. Communications of this type routinely elevate the vision and goals at the heart of the collaboration (the stop sign in the Alinsky exercise) as a touchstone and reminder of the important reason(s) we chose to collaborate in the first place.[4]

External Purposes

Externally, marketing and communications are the attention we pay to how we connect with, project to, and receive information from our external markets. Our tools for projecting the desired image and mission of the collaboration include brochures, publications, press releases, fact sheets, media interviews, and the like. Well-planned and well-managed marketing should accomplish at least three things:

1. It should project the image and mission of the collaboration clearly and effectively. This both shapes the public dialog and serves as a touchstone for the collaboration's members, a statement they can return to when they need to remind themselves or summarize what it is they are doing together.

2. It should generate external support for the work of the collaboration in keeping with its mission and goals.

3. It should frame the successes of the collaboration as the successes of the combined efforts of its institutional members (by name) for both internal and external consumption. This tells the story of the benefits of the collaboration, supports the individual identities and aggregate contributions of its members, and helps maintain the collaboration's momentum.

Technological Savvy

Internet technology makes communication spontaneous, easy, accessible, and cheap. The Internet

- Creates the opportunity for us to share ideas with collaborative partners in the middle of the night or while vacationing on separate continents
- Opens doors to ideas, information, and resources that used to take days or weeks to research
- Enables us to write and plan together even when our schedules don't permit us to be in the same room together
- Puts rules, regulations, and guidelines from government agencies and funding sources in front of us whenever we need them
- Enables event planners and meeting managers to find and compare every calendar that might be relevant
- Creates the opportunity for practitioners to "talk" with each other, get answers to practical how-to questions from each other, find out how others solved looming problems, and find models that have worked for programs that our collaborations may be considering
- Empowers us all with communications resources that we have not yet begun to imagine

Consider the utility of local networks, in which a number of individuals or organizations are linked together on a local server that permits immediate access to shared space on an intranet as well as connections out to the Internet. This enables collaborative partners, individually and collectively, to broadcast and receive information from each other instantaneously. This intranet capacity allows, for example, a defined group of users (the members of the collaboration) to share one secure Web site consisting of the outline of a project proposal to which they each add ideas and edit the ideas of each other at their leisure from their own PCs. Simultaneously, this can permit access to another site on which these same users anywhere in the world can "meet" at a given time every day to chat (correspond live and interactively online) about the work they accomplished that day toward the collaboration's goals.

Let's explore, for a moment, the most profound—and as yet unrealized—implication of information technology on the world of collaboration.

Begin with the concern, lamented most publicly by John F. Kennedy, that public leaders routinely must make decisions without really understanding all the lives that will be affected, all the implications and unforeseen ramifications the decisions will have (he likened this to the unpredictability of ripples created by a stone dropped into a pond).

Now consider the rapid influence information technology has had on transforming the way we do scientific inquiry. The future of technology may well include the death of scientific method as we know it. The tedious, expensive, and time-consuming experimentation that physical and social scientists do, involving the time-honored approach of testing and proving theses-antitheses-syntheses, is a human creation that reflects the limitations of the human intellect (we can only conceive of so many options, hold on to so many facts, think at any one time in a linear or nonlinear fashion, etc.). The growing capacity of information technology enables virtual and spontaneous computer modeling with which scientists can examine all conceivable (and even yet inconceivable) outcomes almost instantaneously. This may very well make the process of hypothesis testing irrelevant . . . and it certainly will enhance public leaders' ability to conceive of (nearly) all the possible implications, interest groups, and organizations that might be affected by—and helpful in—a prospective public project or decision.

With technology's capacity to store and spontaneously share information about individuals and institutions around the world (for example, the work they have done, their institutional missions, programs, scope, and resources) and, of course, to open and maintain easy and ongoing lines of communication, the door is opening to a future that may include the ability of public leaders and scientists to convene comprehensive and universal collaborations.

Most of us are light-years behind the corporate, scientific, and academic elite who, so far, are the primary users and beneficiaries of this technology. But this technology, and the opportunities it offers, are accessible to just about any collaborative leader in any community in the United States. As leaders, it behooves us to understand the potential of this leadership resource, to be competent with the rudiments of how relevant parts of it work, and to build relationships with those who can help us put this technology to work for our collaborative initiatives.

Managerial Skill

Collaborative leaders are called on to be effective and efficient managers of their organizations as well as of their collaborations.

This dimension is self-evident, demands little expansion, and is essential for the survival and success of every collaboration. We, as collaborative leaders, understand the importance of sound management.

Organizational Management

We ensure that our home organizations are well managed so that we can afford to spend the (often-extensive) time needed to build and sustain new collaborations.

Collaborative Management

We make sure that the collaboration itself operates with an air of focused efficiency (in terms of both time and money) and attention to details, finances, and deadlines. We ensure that the cost of participating in the collaboration (in terms of both time and money) never exceeds its obvious benefits from the perspective of each collaborative partner.

One of the most difficult managerial challenges we will face as collaborative leaders is a human relations dilemma made more difficult by the comparative informality and co-equality of our relationships with partners: what to do when a partner must be "fired." Two minds are certainly better than one—which is why we created our collaborations in the first place. But when one mind becomes counterproductive, resistant without legitimate cause for resistance, and drains the resources and threatens the cohesion and survival of the collaboration, then we have three things to consider:

1. The ground rules that should have been established and agreed to by all participants early on. These rules should include language describing what is expected of collaborative partners. It's rare that a collaboration's ground rules will stipulate procedures for removing partners (only a few large and very formal collaborations do), but it is appropriate and comparatively easy to build into the ground rules open and routine evaluations of the effectiveness of the collaboration and of each partner's contribution. (This is a strong indication of why decisions on such matters as ground rules need to be made by consensus and not by a majority vote.)

2. Our persuasive interpersonal skills—our entrepreneurial ability to routinely connect each partner's personal and institutional self-interests to the work of the collaboration—may have failed. Either we didn't make the connection for this person, or this person was beyond connecting. At any rate, having failed at this level, it remains important to save the connection between the collaboration and the institution from which this challenging partner comes. (Toward this end,

questions to ask include, "If there is a higher authority within the home institution, were they aware of the problem? Can the home institution take responsibility for turning this person around? Is it possible that the resistance this person poses is at the direction of the home institution? Is there an underlying cause for concern in the relationship between the institution and the collaboration? Is there an alternate representative that the institution can send to the collaboration?")

3. The final piece of the puzzle in long-term collaborations is to establish alternative structures (such as advisory boards) that offer name recognition and status to members but that have no direct day-to-day involvement in the work of the collaboration. These challenging partners can be graciously and ceremoniously appointed to these alternative structures while their home institutions designate different individuals to serve as institutional representatives to the collaboration.

All this presupposes that we have rigorously and objectively determined that the problem lies in the partner and not in some other—perhaps remediable—element of the collaboration (such as our own leadership or an ill-conceived and dispensable project or direction of the collaboration).

Systems Thinking

Collaborative leaders view their world as the complex interaction of systems: people within organizations within coalitions within communities. . . . The untold ripples that worried President John Kennedy were the unforeseen systems implications of policy decisions he was making.

During the 20th century, management theory evolved from art to science in direct proportion to the emergence of systems theory. From Maslow, the Hawthorn plant, and POSDCORB to Deming, Baldrige, and Peter Senge, we learned the systems within ourselves and our organizations; then we learned the larger systems within which these exist. Today, collaborative leaders take up the challenge of aligning and integrating systems both vertically and horizontally.

This book aims to contribute to the evolution of systems thinking by

• Placing it dead center at the thematic core of collaborative leadership

- Introducing a body of new tools for leading systems through time (the phases of collaboration's life cycle [see Chapter 6, pages 43–51]) and through people (the skills and knowledge of the people who comprise collaborations, described in the 24 dimensions of this chapter and listed in Figure 7.1)
- Persistently reminding readers that the fundamental unit of analysis, influence, and change in any collaborative system is the individual

Chapter 8 proposes a framework for a systems theory of collaboration.

Entrepreneurism

Collaborative leaders are always creating, adapting, and innovating to establish and maintain their relationships with the individuals (Interpersonal Entrepreneurism) and institutions (Institutional Entrepreneurism) in their collaborations.

Interpersonal Entrepreneurism

To be effective collaborative leaders, we use our observations of the psychosocial characteristics of colleagues as tools to shape and direct the relationships we develop with each individual collaborative partner. This entails the ability to connect insight and creativity to

1. Fine-tune and continuously adjust our relationship with each individual in the collaboration to help make sure that each one's evolving self-interests continue to be met

2. Make the most of every opportunity to lead partners into increasingly productive relationships with the collaboration

Institutional Entrepreneurism

Often our success rides on our ability to recognize and take advantage of opportunities to advance the mission we share with our institutional partners. Toward this end,

1. We do the research and ask the questions that help us identify the institutional self-interests of partners (and prospective partners), then develop, evaluate, revise, and refine the connections between institutional self-interests and the mission and goals of the collaboration.

Figure 7.1   Dimensions of Collaborative Leadership

Dimensions of Collaborative Leadership
Strategic thinking Asset-based perspective Professional credibility Timing the launch Recruiting the right mix Interpersonal communication skills Consensus building Diplomacy Understanding the rudiments of each sector Data-driven leadership Psychosocial: understanding people Institutionalizing the worry Group process Resource development Marketing/communications Technological savvy Managerial skill Systems thinking Entrepreneurism Vision-centered leadership Integrity Spirituality Commitment to diversity Charisma

2. As collaborative leaders, we are, by definition, "out-of-the-box" thinkers. Our approach to problem solving and our world-views span the boundaries that constrain most people to persist in looking for solutions within the tried-and-true four walls of their home institutions. Our readiness to straddle borders and step outside the boxes of traditions, norms, organizational constraints, and usual practices also reflects our risk-taking temperament and experimental nature.

The capacity to be entrepreneurial is even more important for us as collaborative leaders than it is for institutional leaders because our effectiveness in the collaboration derives solely from our ability to build, manage, adapt, and maintain the voluntary involvement and commitment of our partners. Let's be direct: If you want to get people to follow you, you either have to own the business that employs them or develop relationships that convince them to voluntarily link their wagons with yours. In public—at least in America's communities and schools—the option doesn't exist to own the enterprise; our ability to lead, interindividually and interinstitutionally, is dependent on our capacity to build responsive and engaging relationships, to strategically influence and organize others. This is relationship management; at the core of relationship management is a behavioral commitment to continuous improvement. The opportunity to lead is given to the person whose image and personality are visible and attractive to those who would follow and whose relationship continues to add value to the self-interest of the individual and/or to the work of the institution. So it follows that to be effective collaborative leaders, we must

1. Develop and employ those people skills and management skills that will increase our visibility and attractiveness in the eyes of current and prospective partners

2. Ensure that every collaborative venture with which we associate holds value-added potential for prospective partners *before* we invite them to join the collaboration

3. Continuously strive to improve the value-added connection of the individual and the collaboration by assessing and addressing indicators of whether the collaboration continues to meet the individual and institutional self-interests of partners

Let's keep in mind the human tendency to understand ourselves only through our reflective interpretation of how others respond to us. That is why a smile or a scowl on the face of a stranger or friend can affect our whole day. If it comes at a moment in which we are ill-formed for the day, it can become our self-assessment. We are not objective; rather, we are the results of the external evaluations that we choose to value. The opposite is also true. In general, the fashion in which people relate to us is largely shaped by their perceptions of us. They are not objective either. Their perceptions are shaped by presumptions and physical stereotypes (ask a short person if they don't find people relating to them as being younger or less mature than would reasonably be expected if they were taller), their prior experiences with people who somehow remind them of you, their prior experiences with you, and the signals and messages that you are sending them at the moment.

As collaborative leaders, we are emphatically aware that our behaviors, and the impressions we make, affect both the perceptions and behaviors of those around us (including their willingness to join in our collaboration). What distinguishes collaborative leaders is that we take responsibility for controlling our behaviors and impressions, recognizing that they are the management and leadership tools we can use to build and influence relationships.

In other words, we need to be savvy behaviorists who understand the process of behavior modification and the extent to which our language, style, and behaviors are the stimuli that generate behavioral responses in those around us. Very few of us have the Machiavellian self-control to strategically plan and execute a regimen of stimuli geared toward generating specific responses in others, and to do so would certainly undermine the humanity and spontaneity of our relationships, which is undesirable. What is important here is the understanding that no one but the collaborative leader has responsibility for the effectiveness of relationships in the collaboration, and therefore, we are responsible for understanding and mastering the relationship-management tools available to us. Moreover, if we feel a relationship within the collaboration is beginning to deteriorate, we don't have the luxury of waiting it out or writing it off; it is our responsibility to strategically adapt and intervene to repair and maintain the relationship (see Box 7.2).

Understanding this element of individual Entrepreneurism is at the core of effective collaborative leadership. The behavioral exchange or interaction that we've been talking about takes place within our relationships. Relationships define the context and opportunities in which we can try to exercise this behavioral influence (this is why I talk of relationship management throughout this book). It is fundamental to an enlightened approach to leadership to understand that *we do not manage people, we manage our relationships with people.* Without a doubt, we are influencing (or attempting to influence) partners' worldviews, interpretations of reality, and choices by negotiating our relationships with them. Fundamentally, relationship management is analogous to the cold-weather game of curling: The best we can do is sweep a path that encourages and makes it easier for the stone (our partner) to move in the direction we desire.

Small-business entrepreneurs manipulate the variables of product quality, price, location, service, and so on, to accomplish their market goals (and collaborative entrepreneurs respect their right to manipulate all the variables at their disposal). We, as collaborative entrepreneurs, intuitively and strategically use our language, behavior, personality, and the like, to create relationships that promote confidence, engagement, and support among collaborative partners to accomplish our strategic goals.

In general, we can operationalize this and make it easier to think about and do, by asking ourselves routinely, "How do we make each individual partner feel?" Do we make our partners feel valued, engaged, rewarded, important, and enthused—or demeaned, superfluous, and taken for granted? When we have the opportunity, do we ask our partners how they feel in the partnership? Do we find ways to discern how they feel about our leadership and style? When such opportunities don't exist, do we do our best to see our relationships in the collaboration through the eyes of each partner? This type of reflection is an important feature of effective collaborations. (See the related discussion that follows, Charisma.)

We've already established that, if we understand the self-interests of the individuals in our collaboration, we have a leg up in our ability to build and maintain relationships that they will find interesting and satisfying. There are many persuasive tactics for doing this. For instance, once you find the fire that burns inside an individual partner, that topic about which the partner simply cannot stop talking (that is, once they have revealed to you an insight to their obvious self-interests), try to weave that topic into the fabric of the organization; use language associated with it in your description of the collaboration's plans and activities. By doing so, you've woven a piece of the partner into the operations of the collaboration and connected the collaboration more securely to that partner's identity and self-interest.

At the root of Entrepreneurism are four elemental characteristics:

1. Creativity

2. Willingness to take risks

3. Willingness to take responsibility

4. Commitment to continuous improvement

Creativity is a great unknown. We assume that people either have it or they don't. But, in the realm of leadership, this isn't true. We can learn to be creative leaders.

In large part, creativity is a listening skill; listening, for example, for good new ideas from others, new insights to partners' individual and institutional self-interests, logical approaches that have not been

Box 7.2   A Note on Maintaining Relationships

On all but the rarest occasions, the relationship is more important than the issue. For the issue-driven, outcomes-oriented types
among us, this may sound counterintuitive, even shocking. But
consider that (1) it will almost never be productive (in your
short- or long-term relationships) to press a partner beyond his
or her self-interest in the collaboration, and (2) each of us in our
lives will have many issues that we will be addressing, each
demanding different partnerships in order to succeed.

   If, in the process of cultivating a relationship for a particular
collaborative campaign, a prospective partner's enthusiasm
wanes beyond repair, he or she gets distracted by institutional or
personal demands, or the direction of the campaign no longer
conforms to the institutional or individual self-interests of the
partner, then it is time to repair to steps of relationship maintenance. In other words, don't simply abandon the relationship
because it is no longer immediately productive; rather, take steps
to effectively put the relationship on hiatus by permitting the
partner to graciously bow out of the collaboration without guilt,
remorse, anger, frustration, or a host of other possible anxieties
and emotions. After doing what it takes to make sure the other
person feels good and comfortable about the communications
and relationship they have begun to enjoy with you, you can
then file their contact information away to be returned to on a
later campaign.

articulated, and holes in logic. This also entails listening for conversations that have not been completed and words that have not been
said. Creativity is, as well, a tenacious resistance to "no" (to the dis-
missive incantations "it can't be done" or "it's never been done that
way") as an answer. Leaders become creative when they persist in
questioning and when they delay the "no." Creative institutions can
be found where leaders avoid the premature "no," where they operate
on the belief that "no" is the answer only after all else has been utterly
exhausted, where you find a dogged determination to find a "yes."

   Risk taking runs parallel with creativity as an essential characteristic of entrepreneurial leaders. We must be comfortable and willing
to make mistakes and tolerant of mistakes made by others. Without
this comfort/willingness/tolerance,

- We lose the opportunity to learn lessons from failed risks since such risks are never taken or such failures are hidden and never explored
- We limit ourselves to doing again only what we know has been successful before and constrain ourselves from ever moving forward to the new and untested ground where collaborative relationships might take us

Can a perfectionist be creative? The answer is "yes," as long as perfection lies in the results and not the process.

Collaborative leaders breed creativity by creating environments that permit, support, encourage, and value the necessary mistakes that will be made on the road to creative solutions. (Great books have never been written without an eraser close at hand.)

Responsibility, within Entrepreneurism, is a straightforward equation: No one but you and me, as collaborative leaders, is responsible for making sure that an answer is found or a problem is solved . . . the buck stops with us. With all our creativity, refusal to accept "no," and recognition that mistakes are steps toward new successes, Entrepreneurism won't happen (new things won't be created) unless we accept responsibility for doing them or for negotiating the relationships necessary to enable us to legitimately hold others accountable for doing them. (See the previous discussion under Institutionalizing the Worry.)

Vision-Centered Leadership

This dimension is clear, simple, and straightforward. In the back of the mind—and on the tip of the tongue—of every collaborative leader is the question, Does this help us achieve our goal(s)? As our collaborations' institutional worriers and strategic thinkers, our job is to ensure that each step our group takes advances us toward our shared goal(s). When our partners wander, get distracted, or slow down, it's up to us to raise the rallying vision like a flag to sustain the focus and momentum of the collaboration. When our coalition is struggling with a problem or over a proposed new direction, our job is to introduce this question as the single most important criterion for making a decision.

But while we keep our partners mindful of the destination we have chosen, collaborative leaders are aware that the best path to get there may not be the shortest, fastest, or cheapest path, or the path of least resistance. The path we take with our partners will be shaped by destination, assets, hurdles, and self-interests. Ultimately, the only right path is the one that reaches the agreed destination.

Integrity

At the foundation of integrity are highly effective "people skills" grounded in obvious and unimpeachable honesty, candor, and dependability.

As collaborative leaders, we have to be trustworthy, otherwise our collaborative partners will not be comfortable sacrificing a little bit of control over their decision making and public image to join our collaboration.

Collaboration is like a marriage with a courtship, during which the intentions and integrity of both parties are tested until each is satisfied that a commitment is safe and warranted. Let's explore this analogy a bit.

We begin with an attraction—whether superficial or soul-deep.

If it's superficial, then we can play. But we both are aware that there is little chance that it will last . . . unless we move to deeper substance. Now, superficial is ok; it can be very satisfying in the short term (like a short-term collaboration).

Let's assume that both parties find the attraction growing stronger; both feel that there may be a future, something good to be gained in this relationship. Up to this point, we have hidden our flaws and projected our strengths. Now, as we spend more time together, we learn more about each other. If we are not blinded by our passions, we measure each other, do research on each other, look for telling missteps, histories that may flag problems, and assets that had been hidden.

At the same time, we judge how the relationship factors into our own needs and future. If we find ourselves believing that the relationship is good—that it satisfies both parties' individual needs and fits in just right with our individual visions—then we begin toying with the big question, "Does each of us trust the other enough to link our futures through sustained collaboration or marriage?"[5]

Institutional leaders agree to follow leaders they trust. They must be confident that in the temporary marriage of the collaboration, their trust will not be abused and their decision to join the collaboration will never be a source of embarrassment.

Effective collaborative leaders never compromise integrity or ethics but recognize that everything else we own or do (language, behavior, even elements of our personality, per the earlier discussion of Entrepreneurism and Charisma) may be tools to be mastered and employed in our efforts to affect how our partners perceive and respond to us. As public leaders, we are challenged to develop and employ the self-knowledge that will enable us to consistently distinguish between those priorities and decisions that we will not flex (those that define our integrity) and all our other characteristics that we are prepared to study, grow, and flex to develop and effectuate the collaborative relationships that are important to us.

At the core of this discussion is an understanding that people who choose to engage in relationships with us (particularly relationships in which we are elevated to some position of leadership relative to them) must be confident in the consistent morality of our behavior and the predictable pattern of our ethics. As public leaders (especially as leaders of leaders within our collaborations), we are each compelled to come to grips with our central defining principles, that is, those values and elements of our character that are central to our identity and self-image.

There is one last point that is especially important for educators and nonprofit leaders. Those of us drawn to leadership in mission-driven public institutions, and especially those of us who would be collaborative leaders within this sector, are held by the public and our colleagues alike to a uniquely high expectation of consistency between our mission-related principles and our behavior. In the past decade alone, we have witnessed the moral lapses of large-city superintendents, a U.S. president, state and federal legislators, teachers in schools across America, and leading philanthropists. The shocking fall of William Aramony, head of the United Way of America, had much less to do with his administrative failings than it did with the lack of consistency between the principles he stood for as leader of the free world's largest philanthropic vehicle, serving the needs of the poor and dispossessed, versus the values he lived as a freewheeling and high-rolling philanderer.

Spirituality

At the soul of optimism is the steadfast belief in the righteousness of our mission . . . effective collaborative leaders project this optimism and help those with whom we work believe it is warranted.

As collaborative leaders, we influence the spirit and worldview of those who join the collaboration. On the surface, we are expected to radiate an energy of achievability—a can-do attitude—that generates a confidence in those around us that the time they are investing will yield the results we all desire.

At a deeper level, we create within our collaborative framework a culture of coherent values, commitment to egalitarian principles, and belief in the Tocquevillian observation that we accomplish more good together than we ever could alone.

A big part of our job is to establish and elevate a shared vision and to make that vision the touchstone for the work done together by collaborative partners. "Where there is no vision," the Bible cautions, "the people perish." It is up to us to keep that vision vital, to routinely and meaningfully connect it to the individual and institutional self-interests of our partners so that they grow individually and advance institutionally. If the vision loses its vitality—or if our partners begin to view the practical day-to-day character of the collaboration as so different from our organizing vision as to make that vision irrelevant—then the collaboration will perish.

Commitment to Diversity

Diversity is not an accomplishment (that is, reaching recruitment and employment percentages that reflect the demographic makeup of a target market), it is a process. Collaborations that don't reflect the diversity of their constituencies in the context of America's sweeping demographic transformation run the immediate and fatal risk of being illegitimate, unresponsive, or worse.

Effective collaborative leaders are adept at spanning boundaries of every type—between sectors, genders, races, religions, ethnicities, and preferences—to bring together those who will be affected by the collaboration and those who can influence the goals of the collaboration. We should make no mistake: The demographic trends of our nation project that to an increasing degree, there is scarcely a public issue worth working on that will not affect diverse constituencies or be controlled by decision makers who do not look or speak like you or me.

A legacy of the past 40 years is that legitimate leadership exists in every identifiable demographic group. There is no need to resort to window dressing; every earnest collaborative leader can find someone within (by that I mean part of) any target population who can represent that population in the collaboration with credibility. To effectively recruit and engage diverse partners in the collaboration, we need to understand the historical and cultural conditions that influence each (prospective) partner. We need to be able to see ourselves and our collaborative issues through the eyes of diverse "others."

To be effective and credible, a collaboration must include, respect, and engage at equal levels representatives from all constituencies affected by the collaborative issue. This level of inclusion, respect, and equity does not have precedent in every community. In many cases, we may find ourselves reaching across racial, religious, and ethnic lines in ways that have not been done before, and our outreach may not always be trusted or well received.

As we broaden our collaboration's membership to represent the full diversity of stakeholders, we have the added duty of building relationships (where none might have been before) with patience, tenacity, and initial focus on those irreducibly common concerns and needs that are important to diverse leaders (that are part of our collective self-interest) and that will assure such leaders that there is good reason for them to sit at a table with us.

As collaborative leaders, we have the additional mandate of examining our own prejudices and stereotypes so as not to be mastered by them, but to master them.

We grow, as collaborative leaders, by learning to see the world through the eyes, traditions, values, and sensibilities of the people around us. This is not simply an idle liberal worldview, it is a practical body of knowledge that makes public leaders more effective.

Charisma

Effective collaborative leaders exude a special type of Charisma that attracts and sustains the emotional desire of others to work with them.

We should never confuse Charisma with dynamism. Charismatic leaders are not necessarily dynamic, although they might be. What makes effective collaborative leaders charismatic is the ability to attract and sustain the emotional desire of other people to want to work with them—to like working with them. It is connected to integrity, dependability, and a general can-do optimism but is really an affective quality that is hard to define and can only be observed —and, therefore, taught—through the eyes of other people. Either people want to work with you and like working with you . . . or they don't!

Those of us who aren't born with the inherent ability to be loved by all have to find ways to see ourselves and our behaviors through the eyes of others. These "others"—whether they be friends, mentors, coworkers, or other types of "informants"—are the mirrors that enable us to see ourselves, assess our own abilities to attract and sustain the personal and emotional commitments of others, and practice the development of our charismatic skills.

Box 7.3   Criticism as a Tool of Relationship Management

Dealing with criticism—as the provider or the recipient—may be one of the best examples of a natural element of our relationships with other people that may cause them to view us as easy or difficult—desirable or undesirable—to work with.

In the extremely rare instance when criticizing someone becomes necessary, the act of criticizing will become a defining moment in our relationship with that person. It can change the temperament and balance of the relationship . . . or it can solidify the relationship by contributing to a shared sense of open and honest communication, helping to transform incompatible behaviors, and confirming our qualities as people who lead well and work well with others. Here are some practical suggestions:

- Criticism we deliver should always be constructive; couched in the context of both the acknowledged positive attributes of the person being criticized, a clear enunciation of the negative impacts of the criticized behavior, and specific recommendations for remedying the criticized behavior.

- As the recipient of criticism, we should recognize that in most cases, our critic is either uncomfortable or emotionally strained when delivering the message; putting him or her at ease with the good-natured and constructive fashion in which the criticism is received will go a long way to cementing a constructive relationship. We should solicit sufficient details so that the criticism is thoroughly understood. Acknowledge the effect that the criticized behavior has or had on that partner. And establish a dialog with the partner in which recommended remediations are solicited and shared. We should discuss a final strategy for resolving the problem. Where possible, we should engage the relationship partner in the problem-solving remediation.

A leader can have all the behavioral self-knowledge and relationship management skills previously described in the section, Entrepreneurism, but without Charisma, this leader is like a lead-footed ballroom dancer with all the right moves and none of the essential grace and believability. In other words, if we give the impression of being driven toward outcomes and fail to get our partners to feel good about our collaborative relationships with them —or if we are viewed as slick, manipulative, intemperate, not comfortable around people, or not comfortable to be with—then our efforts to be collaborative leaders will fail despite our mastery of all the other dimensions outlined in this chapter.

Charismatic qualities are extremely hard to develop. First, we have to see them. This is the hardest step. We can ask our friends (and even folks we barely know) to help us understand what it is about us that encourages or discourages others from joining us. We can watch ourselves on tape (like a television reporter) and try to see ourselves as others see us and capture what appears to work in our visual and aural presentations. Then we can learn to imitate certain examples of Charismatic behavior that eventually, after repetition, may insinuate themselves into our character.

Notes

1. The most articulate proponents of asset-based leadership are John McKnight and John Kretzmann, leading the way with their book *Building Communities From the Inside Out: A Path Toward Finding and Mobilizing a Community's Assets.*

2. To model this efficiency, I refer you to the work of Marleen C. Pugach and Lawrence J. Johnson, *Collaborative Practitioners, Collaborative Schools* (1995), and Peter Senge et al., *Schools That Learn* (2000), which devote substantial space to the relationship of communication and collaboration.

3. In fact, within the collaboration, it may well be advisable for the leader to never take credit at all but to dole it out as a tool for building the sense of ownership and involvement of our collaborative partners. (Being publicly credited for something you thought about but didn't do will leave you wondering forever whether you did or said something that had greater influence than you had imagined. I know, I've been on both sides of this equation!)

4. During the building year of the Ohio Learning First Alliance, a continuously growing electronic record that included the Alliance's mission, goals, and major decisions made at each meeting was emailed to all partners after each meeting.

5. This analogy can continue with relevant parallels to collaborative leadership: moving beyond the courtship into the process of building the relationship, of enjoying and reinforcing those elements that overlap between the partners and of adapting individually so as to accommodate each other. In this process, which is the ongoing process of both love and relationship management, key benchmarks and events become essential elements around which the relationship is grown (e.g., the first kiss, the engagement ring, the wedding, and more, are paralleled in events and activities in the collaboration). Of course, separation and divorce are also unfortunate options in this analogy with romance and love—as is reconciliation—which all have their parallels in the course of collaboration as well.

8

A Framework for Future Study

W e are building our understanding of collaboration together. Teachers, parents, administrators, researchers, theoreticians, and students all have something to contribute to this developing conversation.

This book has added the phases of collaboration's life cycle and the skills and knowledge of collaboration's dimensions to our work together. This summary chapter introduces a theoretical framework that connects these elements in an integrated system of collaboration.

As a theoretical framework, all that follows needs to be tested. Practitioners need to determine whether this framework helps us succeed in our roles as collaborative leaders. Researchers need to go inside this design to establish its coherence as a framework and its validity as a collection of theories.

We begin by grounding this theoretical framework in the widely adopted principles of Quality systems.

Connecting the Principles

It used to be said that leadership is leadership is leadership . . . and, in a fundamental way, who is to say that's not true? While sectors define the context, purpose, and even priorities of what leaders do, a genuinely good leader in one field stands a very good chance of generating a good following in any other field. In similar fashion, it makes little sense for us to think that the leadership skills of an effective collaborator in the field of education vary widely from those that would be found in an effective collaborative leader in government, business, or the nonprofit sector.

In these other sectors, Quality principles have emerged as the prevailing construct for discussing, assessing, teaching, and learning how to lead systems. In one form or another, with modifications of language, the seven Quality principles outlined in Chapter 5 repeat throughout leadership literature and practice and constitute the prevailing knowledge. It is no wonder, although belated, that these principles are emerging with popularity as the style of new leaders and practitioners in public education.

John Dewey taught us that the best way to teach is to connect new knowledge to the heritage or base of skills and facts that already exist within the learner. Because our aim—as we write and read this book—is to generate new knowledge and skills regarding the roles, content, practice, and theory of collaboration, our teaching will be more effective, accepted, and widely understood if we attach it to the prevailing knowledge of Quality systems and principles.

Table 8.1 offers a shorthand for this attachment, connecting the seven Quality principles to the 12 phases of collaboration's life cycle. The table extends this attachment by connecting the skills and knowledge ("dimensions") of collaboration in clusters under each of the seven Quality principles. By suggesting a definitional linkage between Quality principles and collaboration's dimensions, this table invites practitioners and scholars to

- Interpret Quality through the lens of collaboration
- Explore collaboration's dimensions as a tool for implementing Quality systems alignment

The exercise of matching Quality principles and collaboration's dimensions does not yield a perfect fit. As the chart reflects, 20 of the dimensions easily align and offer clarity and help in operationalizing the principles. Four dimensions cluster together quite well but do not easily attach to any Quality principle. What does this mean?

Integrity, Spirituality, Commitment to Diversity, and Charisma cluster together within a rubric I have titled Character. I offer this as the missing principle—the human element that is essential for influencing people within systems. Every experienced Quality practitioner knows that *sustained* systems alignment can never be done *to* people

Table 8.1

Principles of Quality Leadership	Dimensions of Collaborative Leadership
Leadership	Strategic thinking
	Asset-based perspective
	Professional credibility
Strategic Planning	Timing the launch
	Recruiting the right mix
Stakeholder Focus	Interpersonal communication skills
	Consensus building
	Diplomacy
	Understanding the rudiments of each sector
Fact-Based Decision Making	Data-driven leadership
Sensitivity to Human Resources	Psychosocial: understanding people
	Institutionalizing the worry
Managerial Systems	Group process
	Resource development
	Marketing/communications
	Technological savvy
	Managerial skill
Continuous Improvement	Systems thinking
	Entrepreneurism
	Vision-centered leadership
Character	Integrity
	Spirituality
	Commitment to diversity
	Charisma

within a system but only *with* them. By adding Character to the Quality lexicon, we emphasize the principle that change occurs through individual relationships. These individual relationships both occur within and influence change inside the larger system. By adding Character, we move Quality practices beyond the traditional assumption that change occurs only in systems, departments, and other clusters of people . . . it also pays strategic attention to influencing change in the individual.

By attaching new thought and lessons of collaboration to Quality principles, it should be easier and more palatable for leaders, researchers, practitioners, and evaluators to view collaboration as a collection of realistic tools for aligning Quality systems. By comparing the principles of Quality and dimensions of collaboration, we strengthen our knowledge of both,

- Yielding a more rigorous framework and logic for understanding collaboration's dimensions
- Adding new dimensions and tools to the evolving world of Quality in schools, government, businesses, and service agencies

A Challenge for Readers

This book is sprinkled with theory, but it's not theoretical. It is framed to make you think, but it's not scholarly. It propels us toward collaboration in how we lead our schools and districts, how we teach in public schools, and what we teach our teachers and children, but it's more than a call to action. And it diagrams the life cycle of collaboration and describes the skills and knowledge that make collaboration work, but it's not a recipe to be followed step-by-step.

This is a book intended to open new pathways to collaboration, new tools, new research, new thinking, new advocates, and better leaders. It is intended to help you make a difference in your work, community, and the life of a child. If it sits on your shelf and never spurs you to action, to better leadership, or to better teaching, then I've pushed the string and you've let it lie, and I have failed to make the connection.

So I challenge each of you to find at least a piece of this book that you can carry forward into meaningful action.

Table 8.2 A Theoretical Framework for Collaborative Leadership

Principles of Quality Leadership	Dimensions of Collaborative Leadership	Phases of Collaboration's Life Cycle												
		Why collaborate?	Outcomes?	Decision makers?	Stakeholders?	Frame and recruit	Leaders, structure, roles, & rules	Develop action plan	Begin with success	Build bonds between partners	Celebrate successes	Assess, adjust, reinforce bonds	Goal-centered accountability	Revisit & renew mission
Leadership	Strategic thinking													
	Asset-based perspective													
	Professional credibility													
Strategic Planning	Timing the launch													
	Recruiting the right mix													
Stakeholder Focus	Interpersonal communication skills													
	Consensus building													
	Diplomacy													
	Understanding the rudiments of each sector													
Fact-Based Decision Making	Data-driven leadership													
Sensitivity to Human Resources	Psychosocial: understanding people													
	Institutionalizing the worry													
Managerial Systems	Group process													
	Resource development													
	Marketing/communications													
	Technological savvy													
	Managerial skill													
Continuous Improvement	Systems thinking													
	Entrepreneurism													
	Vision-centered leadership													
Character	Integrity													
	Spirituality													
	Commitment to diversity													
	Charisma													

A Special Challenge for Researchers, Scholars, Evaluators, and Trainers

Ours is the job of advancing understanding, skills, and knowledge. Table 8.2 represents a theoretical framework of collaborative leadership, integrating the new thoughts presented in the last two chapters. It's been discussed, and anecdotally applied, but never tested, neither as a coherent whole nor as a matrix of cells, each of which introduces challengeable theories. So challenge it. Test it. Kick its tires . . . hard. Make the work presented here the beginning of a partnership in advancing the skills, knowledge, understanding, and science of collaborative leadership.

9

Seven Nuggets

A Practitioner's Postscript

Nearly every author of nonfiction books is routinely asked for a thumbnail version of their work (a brief synopsis of the most salient lessons), asked, one can only assume, by people who would rather not have to buy the book.

I had an undergraduate professor who once told me that if you can't summarize big thoughts into practical bite-size nuggets, then you haven't really learned something worth teaching. So I take the thumbnail inquiries as a personal challenge and make it a practice to make it easy for those readers who skip to the back of a book looking for the few salient nuggets.

The following seven principles represent some of the most essential elements found time and time again in collaborations that work. They are not a summary, or even a comprehensive overview, but they are exceptionally important. And if you leave this book with only these points ringing in your consciousness, then the odds are you will be on the road to being an effective collaborative leader.

Seven Principles of Effective Collaborative Leadership

1. Cultivate a *shared vision* right from the start ... even if it's vague.

2. Take care to *recruit the right mix* to reach your stakeholders and decision makers.

3. Become—or ensure you've identified—the *institutional worry*. This is the person who will pay unwavering attention to
   - Sustaining the momentum and attending to the management details of the collaboration
   - Engaging the perspectives and addressing the process needs of each individual partner in the work of the collaboration

4. To the greatest extent possible, ensure that each partner's individual and institutional *self-interests are served* by both the process and products of the collaboration.

5. *Don't waste time*. Meetings must be efficient and productive; management must be lean and driven. Remember that for everyone else, this is no more than a second priority.

6. *Routinize the structure and the roster of participants.* Make the collaboration a regular item on participants' schedules.
   - Develop clear roles and responsibilities for participants (even if these roles and responsibilities regularly shift among partners).
   - Recognize that it is easier and more popularly received to cancel a meeting or remove a responsibility than it is to add a meeting or responsibility to participants' lives.
   - Secure commitments from all participants that every human effort will be made to ensure that the same people come to the table each time the collaboration meets—scarcely anything stifles creativity, productivity, and commitment more than wasting time each meeting bringing a new delegate "up to speed."

7. *All collaboration is personal.*
   - Cultivating partners shouldn't end once they commit to the partnership. Cultivation of partners' attachment to the collaboration requires ongoing attention.
   - "Interinstitutional collaboration" is a common misnomer. Effective collaboration happens b*etween people—one person at a time.*

References

Alinsky, S. D. (1971). *Rules for radicals: A pragmatic primer for realistic radicals.* New York: Vintage Books.

De Pree, M. (1993). *Leadership Jazz: The art of conducting business through leadership, followership, teamwork, voice, touch.* New York: Dell.

deTocqueville, A. (1981). *Democracy in America.* New York: Random House. (original publication 1962)

McKnight, J., & Kretzmann, J. (1993). *Building communities from the inside out: A path toward finding and mobilizing a community's assets.* Chicago: ACTA Publications.

Pugach, M. C., & Johnson, L. J. (1995). *Collaborative practitioners collaborative schools.* Denver, CO: Love Publishing Company.

Rubin, H. (1998). *Collaboration skills for educators and nonprofit leaders.* Chicago: Lyceum Books.

Senge, P., Cambron-McCabe, N., Lucas, T., Smith, B., Dutton, J., & Kleiner, A. (2000). *Schools that learn: A fifth discipline fieldbook for educators, parents, and everyone that cares about education.* New York: Doubleday.

Slaughter-Defoe, D. T., & Rubin, H. (2001). A longitudinal case study of Head Start-eligible children: Implications for urban education. *Educational Psychologist, 36*(1), 31–44.

Index

THE STORY OF PENGUIN CLASSICS

Before 1946 . . . "Classics" are mainly the domain of academics and students; readable editions for everyone else are almost unheard of. This all changes when a little-known classicist, E. V. Rieu, presents Penguin founder Allen Lane with the translation of Homer's *Odyssey* that he has been working on in his spare time.

1946 Penguin Classics debuts with *The Odyssey,* which promptly sells three million copies. Suddenly, classics are no longer for the privileged few.

1950s Rieu, now series editor, turns to professional writers for the best modern, readable translations, including Dorothy L. Sayers's *Inferno* and Robert Graves's unexpurgated *Twelve Caesars.*

1960s The Classics are given the distinctive black covers that have remained a constant throughout the life of the series. Rieu retires in 1964, hailing the Penguin Classics list as "the greatest educative force of the twentieth century."

1970s A new generation of translators swells the Penguin Classics ranks, introducing readers of English to classics of world literature from more than twenty languages. The list grows to encompass more history, philosophy, science, religion, and politics.

1980s The Penguin American Library launches with titles such as *Uncle Tom's Cabin* and joins forces with Penguin Classics to provide the most comprehensive library of world literature available from any paperback publisher.

1990s The launch of Penguin Audiobooks brings the classics to a listening audience for the first time, and in 1999 the worldwide launch of the Penguin Classics Web site extends their reach to the global online community.

The 21st Century Penguin Classics are completely redesigned for the first time in nearly twenty years. This world-famous series now consists of more than 1,300 titles, making the widest range of the best books ever written available to millions—and constantly redefining what makes a "classic."

The Odyssey continues . . .

The best books ever written

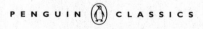

PENGUIN ( ) CLASSICS

SINCE 1946

Find out more at www.penguinclassics.com

Visit www.vpbookclub.com